CW01511462

Brian Harris provides an insightful approach to leadership development by encouraging prospective leaders to consider how they are formed and shaped for the role. This is a timely book as the rhythms, disciplines and approaches which bring about deep transformation are often neglected or overlooked in contemporary literature. Brian advocates for a balance of competence and character in leadership development. In doing so, he challenges the popular model of the heroic, charismatic leader and encourages the valuing of authenticity, humility, sacrifice and service.

*Dr Daniel Pampuch, CEO of Christian Schools Australia*

I am most grateful that Brian Harris has written this book, which I expect will be read and studied by Christian leaders and leadership teams across the globe. It offers rich insights that will challenge, inspire and equip a new generation of leaders. The principles contained in it have the potential to be transformative for leaders and bring health and vitality to the communities being served.

*Dr Graeme Cross, CEO of Swan Christian Education Association, Australia*

Harris' *Stirrers and Saints* searches for the elusive profile of a Christian leader whose character is earthed in godliness and a spirit of restlessness and discontent, who refuses to settle for mediocrity and a tepid status quo. With refreshing clarity, practical self-assessment charts and reflective questions, he explores the convergence of a robust spiritual formation with the evolution of the Christian leader. A book I needed to read fifty years ago!

*Prof. David Crutchley, dean of the School of Biblical and Theological Studies, Carson-Newman University*

If *Stirrers and Saints: Forming spiritual leaders of skill, depth and character* had been available four decades ago, I would have been a better leader. I would have reflected more deeply, had a greater understanding of myself and empathy for those I was leading, and led with not just more competence but confidence. Every word Brian writes, resonates. Many of the insights he shares have been hard-won lessons in my own leadership journey and there are so many things I wish I had known earlier. Not just I would have benefited, but those in my sphere of influence too. My contribution to the kingdom of God would have been greater. As I lay down Brian's book, there are so many things I ache to have enough time left to put into practice and to encourage and nurture within myself, and in those I have the privilege to lead at this later stage in my ministry. May the inspiration and wisdom of this work not just continue to change me and many, but also the substance and trajectory of leadership in and through the church.

*Melissa Lipsett, CEO of Baptist World Aid /*
*Transform Aid International, Australia*

*Stirrers and Saints* is a leadership degustation experience with a master sage chef. Brian Harris carefully presents tastings of what deeply matters in leadership in our time. As you read, you, like I, will begin to realize you are engaging the signature dish of the sage chef. Quiet, tenacious, holy, humble leadership. You will find you are both comforted and challenged and hope is left in your soul. Probably you won't notice just when or where that happened.

*Revd Monica O'Neil, pastoral supervisor*
*and founder of The Anchorage Collective*

# Stirrers and Saints

## Forming spiritual leaders of skill, depth and character

### Brian Harris

Paternoster:
thinking faith

First published 2024 by Paternoster
Paternoster is an imprint of Authentic Media Ltd
PO Box 6326, Bletchley, Milton Keynes MK1 9GG.
authenticmedia.co.uk

**British Library Cataloguing in Publication Data**
A catalogue record for this book is available from the British Library
ISBN 978-1-78893-360-5
978-1-78893-361-2 (e-book)

Cover design by Henry Milne
Printed and bound by CPI Group (UK) Ltd, Croydon, CR0 4YY

One of the great joys of my life is getting to work with the staff and clients of AVENIR Leadership Institute. This book is dedicated to them, in gratitude for the difference we get to make in the world.

# Contents

# Foreword

I first met Dr Brian Harris when he came to London on a well-earned research sabbatical. Brian and his wife Rosemary stayed at one of Spurgeon's College's apartments. The plan was for Brian to engage in research, do a few lectures on leadership and ministerial formation at the College and for him and his wife to enjoy visiting friends in London and the amazing opportunities a global city like London affords. I was in my first year as the Principal of Spurgeon's College, after resigning my commission in the Royal Army Chaplains' Department. In contrast, Brian was a hugely experienced Principal of Vose Seminary, Perth, Australia. Despite the contrast in experience, Brian was gracious and encouraging; he also asked some penetrating questions, which I found incredibly helpful.

As I read *Stirrers and Saints*, its themes were familiar to me. Perhaps this is because the book had its origins at Spurgeon's. A more likely reason is the numerous conversations we had together, in which it was clear Brian had a passion to provide pastors and ministers with accessible resources to become better leaders, while simultaneously growing in spiritual maturity. The Higher Education and Research Act, also known as HERA, became law in the UK in 2017. This Act radically transformed the higher educational landscape in which theological colleges like Spurgeon's would operate. The question facing every Bible college in England, was how they would respond to the implications of HERA. I remember the gracious but incisive questions Brian asked me about the challenge to change while at the same time remaining consistent in the mission of training women and men for Christian mission, ministry and leadership in the con-temporary world. This is summed up in chapter 1: 'someone willing to stir things up a little and champion change, but someone who also stays close to Jesus.'

What I enjoyed about this book is the obvious intention of the author to provide resources that will be helpful to those in Christian leadership. The three parts of *Stirrers and Saints* take readers on a logical journey from Section A which explores spiritual formation, through Section B, focusing upon examples of biblical leadership (Moses, Daniel and Mary), to Section C, with its emphasis upon leadership and in particular quiet leadership, rather than charismatic models of leadership. Dr Harris' breadth of experience, especially in the endeavour to form spiritual leaders, infuses this work with an honesty and humility, which I believe will resonate with readers. Chapter 5, 'Formed by Conflict, Disappointment and Failure', has a vitally important concept that I have personally wrestled with in over 30 years of ministry; 'not everything finishes in triumph, and that how we travel the journey of failure can be even more impor-tant than how we travel the journey of success.' Depression, shame, tragedy and false accusation are the unwelcome expressions of reality that every leader, who ever built or achieved anything of spiritual significance, will be all too familiar with. The biblical examples ex-plored will give readers a balanced and refreshing insight into the lives of familiar heroes of the faith.

Across the decades, alumni of Spurgeon's College are frequently associated with the practice of alliteration. Seeing the 'Seven S Inventory' of leadership made me smile but also piqued my curios-ity. They do work and are not strained. My sense is that readers will enjoy how 'Stirrer, Saint, Servant, Shepherd, Steward, See-er and Sage' is unpacked and explored. I completely agreed with Dr Harris when he says, 'The Church is facing a leadership vacuum. Many of our leaders have led from muddled motives and we are paying the price. While we should lament what has gone wrong, we must also learn from it.' Looking back over thirty years in Christian ministry,

I recognise that a deep unease exists among some ministerial colleagues about describing the minister / pastor as a leader; this disquiet is extended to the use of the word leadership in a Christian context. When, however, readers reflect upon the Seven S Inventory, I strongly suspect that they will agree with its tone and content. The problem, as I see it, is that good, godly leadership is, far too often, not the norm. When Christians encounter it, they find it attractive and compelling. I am convinced that leaders can be grown, and that leadership is something that can be nurtured and developed, if there is a humble spirit, a willingness to evolve and a hunger to reach one's God given potential. I have known Brian Harris for a number of years now and his desire to continue to learn and grow is evidenced in his honest reflection upon his own journey. *Stirrers and Saints* has a richness to it precisely because it is drawn from years of experience and a genuine desire to share hard-earned insights over many years in ministry and leadership with those who have a similar, honest desire to grow and develop as godly leaders. This book is 'about forming stirrers and saints, spiritual leaders who will guide and inspire those who follow them to dream more boldly, live more courageously and follow Jesus more faithfully.' My prayer is that the family of God will be blessed by those who read this insightful book and become Stirrers and Saints.

*Revd Prof. Philip P. McCormack, MBE*
*Principal and Vice-Chancellor, Spurgeon's College, London*

# Preface

I have written several books, but I suspect this is the most important. The Christian church has its fair share of charismatic leaders. Some have huge and adoring followings they manage to entertain while passing on nuggets of lasting value. But often you sense that though they are classified as spiritual leaders and might be able to lead their church to dizzy heights, they are not really guides you can trust for the spiritual journey. Not the real, deep, heart-wrenching stuff that life requires us to face, the inner soul-work that has no quick fixes. All too often we hear of the spectacular demise of one of these leaders, a victim not of a terrible, life-terminating disease, but of falling for common-or-garden sins like lust, and greed, and power and deceit. Sadly I no longer feel shocked when I hear the news. Sometimes I have had the sense that it was not a case of *if* I would hear of the fall, but *when* I would hear of it. The emptiness of the person's soul has been as obvious as that.

If our leaders are sometimes not sound spiritual guides, there is another side to the equation. Some of our spiritual guides are not really leaders – or not in the sense that people follow where they go, or that they have clear and worthy goals that they, through working together with others, achieve.

The irony is this. Those who have the most to say sometimes say it to the smallest audiences. Those whose lives are worth copying are often unnoticed. There are worthy spiritual guides, but they do not know how to lead.

Sometimes the fault is ours, for we insist on drinking at the well of superficiality. We might get the leaders we deserve because we are passive followers and are not constructive participants in the journey we are on.

But that is not always the case.

Sometimes those who should say the most do not know how to say it, and those who have the most to offer do not know how to make the offer known. They could learn; it's just that they haven't.

I have been training people for spiritual leadership for several decades and have become increasingly convinced that we need to look at the two sides of the equation – both spiritual formation and leadership. We need leaders who are simultaneously stirrers and saints, leaders who will not settle for the status quo and who are unafraid to ruffle feathers, but who, despite their busy schedule, are godly people whose well runs deep. Leaders who are also saints.

Now there are many dangers along this route, for leadership poses real threats to the soul. It usually comes with a measure of power over others, and power can be intoxicating. It can corrode the soul. Leaders must learn the art of compromise, and cynicism can result from that. We can sometimes forget what we stand for. Leaders are usually looked up to by their followers, and how can you remain humble when most people are telling you that you are exceptional?

It is foolish not to acknowledge these risks, and some quietly avoid them by abandoning the leader inside themselves. If you do not travel the leadership road, you can avoid the temptations it brings.

But there is another peril, and the church is reeling because we have not adequately acknowledged it. Spiritual guides may leave leadership to those who long for leadership and often proclaim their own leadership ability. In abandoning the leadership space to those who have not deeply nurtured their souls, those who are more spiritually mature empower superficial and silly spokespeople to represent the Christian faith to the world. The strident and confident hollowness of these 'leaders' is usually apparent to most, which explains why a watching world no longer considers the church a refuge for the soul and a place for spiritual growth. The tragedy of this should break our hearts.

I hope that in some small measure this book will help to bridge this worrying divide and that in the future we will have a growing number of genuine spiritual guides who lead us well through the ever-changing challenges of the twenty-first century. It is not accidental that the book starts with reflections on nurturing the soul. Nor is it accidental that it finishes with reflections on leadership – for the well-nurtured soul will still hear the voice of God asking: 'Whom shall I send? And who will go for us?' It should soberly reply, 'Here am I. Send me!' (Isa. 6:8).

*Brian Harris*

# Acknowledgements

This book was written over a period of five years, a longer time than I anticipated; but then, life has many unexpected turns, and in this case the global Covid-19 pandemic was one of them. I started writing it in 2018 when on a half sabbatical from Vose Seminary, which I spent at Spurgeon's College in London. It was an idyllic setting in which to research, think and dream, and I am deeply grateful to the staff and students who went out of their way to welcome me and my wife Rosemary. I am especially grateful to Spurgeon's principal, the Revd Prof. Philip McCormack, who had recently started his tenure at the college, and generously gave of his time and insights as we chatted our way through church politics, theology, leadership and theological education. We have kept in touch and I am delighted that Philip has written the foreword.

My plan had been to finish the book during the second half of my sabbatical, which I spent as a visiting professor at Carson Newman University in the USA. The year was 2020 – need I say more? Everything had been going exceptionally well, I was teaching and writing, and Prof. David Crutchley and his staff had made me feel fully at home. And then Covid-19, and suddenly Rosemary and I were desperately searching for a flight back to Australia. It turned out fine, and I am most grateful for the assistance provided by Carson Newman, but it meant my writing schedule was completely thrown out as I had to return to lead a theological college making the endless adjustments that were required during the Covid-19 era. There were many rich learnings during that time, and I am grateful now for the delays, as I think the book is the richer for them, and has been able to incorporate some of the lessons from that complex period.

A merger of Vose Seminary with Morling College followed, and the seminary where I was principal for seventeen years is now the Vose Campus of Morling College, undoubtedly one of the finest theological colleges in the Southern Hemisphere. It has been a privilege to be associated with the merger, and to see the many new opportunities it has opened for students. Morling College generously provided me with time to finish writing this book, and I am grateful to them.

I've dedicated *Stirrers and Saints* to the staff of AVENIR Leadership Institute. With my time at Vose Seminary drawing to a close, I and two friends decided to form AVENIR to help train the leaders we believe the world needs. We have been running for three years, the team has expanded and each year has seen significant growth. More importantly, we have been able to host and participate in rich and necessary discussions with thousands of current and emerging leaders. They are stirrers and saints, people who are making a difference in the varied contexts and countries in which they work. Leading AVENIR is more than an honour. It is a source of joy and delight as the team nudges me towards new ways of thinking and fresh ways of interacting with the world. From deep within me I say thank you.

My family is always supportive of my endeavours and I want to note how much that means to me. My son-in-law, Dr Aaron Chidgzey, has gone out of his way to provide help, and with the insights he has gained from his engaging 'Isms and Schisms' podcast, has guided me in the production of the Stirrers and Saints podcast which supplements this book. Thanks Aaron.

This is my fifth Paternoster book. I keep coming back to them as their staff go more than the extra mile in the support, encouragement and practical guidance they provide. My sincere thanks to them.

# Introduction

Therefore be as shrewd as snakes and as innocent as doves.

*Matt. 10:16*

'You can't have it all,' he said. 'Yes, it would be nice for this church to be led by someone with quaintly saint-like qualities, but what we need now is strong leadership. There are financial challenges, staffing challenges and issues with morale. Add to that, we've no real vision about where we're going or what we're trying to do. What we need is a leader. Someone who is a stirrer. Someone who will get things moving. If they are a spiritual giant, wonderful, and if not – well, so be it. The non-negotiable is leadership because everything stands or falls on leadership.'

'You can't have it all.' The phrase has stuck in my mind. Is it too much to hope that our churches would be led by people who are models of spiritual integrity and life, but who also know how to lead well? Spiritual leaders who are both stirrers and saints. On hearing the scepticism, I instinctively want to reject it as outrageous, a silly false dichotomy which suggests that leaders can't be godly and that godly people can't be leaders.

While it is one thing to reject a proposal because it is not to your liking, it is another to coldly analyse it and to ask if it has some validity. As I did so, I came to the reluctant conclusion that while the case is a little overstated, in too many instances it seems to be true. I can think of ever so many churches that are led by godly pastors who are ministering to smaller and smaller congregations. Many of them provide a wonderful example of what it means to be a Christ-like person. They are unselfish and willing to give themselves up for the good of others. But their churches are in decline, and there is no plan in place for the present, let alone any vision for the future. Godly they may be, but leaders they are not.

By contrast I can think of some thriving churches that have all kinds of ethical questions hanging over them. Too many staff members have been burnt out, attendance figures have been exaggerated, and anyone brave enough to ask questions about this is quickly shown the door. There is unease over the way money is used and power distributed. People ask if the end justifies the means but are shamed into silence as the church appears to be ever more successful. If results are measured in terms of attendance and giving, these are effective churches. However, for all the outward appearance of success, deep in your heart you know the leader would never stand by you in a crisis, especially if you had ever challenged anything they wanted to do. Leaders they are, but valid spiritual guides they are not.[1]

This is an issue I grappled with in the seventeen years I led a theological seminary, training people to be pastors, chaplains, and leaders of mission organizations. I continue to explore it as I now head a leadership institute. I am deeply conscious that the Christian faith today faces three significant challenges, in that it is widely portrayed to be intellectually vacuous, morally suspect and experientially empty. Put differently, people increasingly doubt that Christianity is true, moral or relevant.[2] As I have participated in the training of thousands of people for Christian leadership, I have had to ask if the training we offer provides graduates with the necessary intellectual rigour to face the challenges that lie ahead. And I have had to ask if we provide sufficient nurture to shape their moral formation so that they become genuinely virtuous individuals – ones in whom people see something of the likeness of Jesus. And I have had to ask if our graduates are sufficiently strong and imaginative to be able to lead the churches and missional endeavours they oversee to new and exciting paths of faithfulness, relevance and engagement.

While this book only lightly explores the development of an intellectually rigorous faith, it dives into the other two areas. How is genuine virtue formed inside people – formed in such a way that it becomes an instinctive default, such that when they act against it they automatically feel uncomfortable and aware that something is amiss? And can this be linked to spiritual sensitivity, such that people are open to the ongoing guidance and voice of God in their life, and are mindful of and attuned to what God is saying to them and showing them? Can people formed in this way learn leadership skills so that their virtue overflows for the greater good, as they become genuine servant leaders, who shepherd and steward the people and resources God entrusts to them for significant impact?

Put differently, how do we go about forming spiritual leaders?

As I write this sentence I am conscious that each of the three key words in the question is important: forming . . . spiritual . . . leaders.

Forming reflects a conviction that there is no simple formula to be mastered or found. A short course in spiritual maturity supplemented by another in leadership will not do it. Formation is life long and life wide. And though we are never fully formed, we can be on journeys that either deepen our formation or undermine it. We can approach life with enlightened eyes, eyes observant of both the opportunities and the hazards we encounter. It is possible to understand and put in place practices that are likely to deepen us, just as it is possible to implement practices likely to sabotage our growth. Section A of this book explores a range of formational practices that will serve us for the long term – life-serving practices that will see us continuing to grow, well beyond any arbitrary retirement age.

Section B asks what sets a spiritual leader apart from other leaders. We'll look at some leaders in the Bible – often with flaws, to be sure, but nevertheless people whose leadership flowed from a deep commitment to lead for the cause and work of God. This helps to earth our reflection, for each of the three we study (Moses, Daniel and Mary) lived real lives and faced genuine challenges and overwhelming complexity, yet somehow managed to emerge as both stirrer and saint. We can learn a lot from each of them.

Section C then explores steps to take to ensure that our formation and deepening spiritual maturity finds a constructive and life-serving outlet in leadership. I have written previously about quiet leadership and will unpack some quiet leadership principles that can help even reluctant leaders to become increasingly effective as they realize that leadership is not primarily about charisma but more about having a settled sense of direction and vision and systematically, patiently and tenaciously working to achieve it.[3]

The book's conclusion then draws these three strands together.

My hope, indeed my prayer, is that as you read this book you will not think what a great idea this is for unnamed others, but that God will nudge you into realizing that this is for you – and that wherever it is that God wants to use you, you are being called to be both a stirrer and a saint, someone formed for spiritual leadership.

It was 1997. I had been pastoring Mt Roskill Baptist Church in Auckland, New Zealand, for a little over two years. God had been good to us, and the church was growing steadily – so steadily that we faced the problem of many churches in this position. How were we to accommodate the ever-increasing number of people who wanted to be part of what God was doing there?

There were two obvious answers. We could either enlarge our facilities or add a second Sunday morning service. We also briefly considered planting a new congregation but felt that we needed critical mass for some of the things God was calling us to, so we put that option aside. As we grappled with the 'enlarge the buildings' or 'start a second morning service' question, the leadership wisely recognized that this was not a matter to settle simply by debate and long lists of positives and negatives. We called the church to prayer and fasting, and agreed on a listening process to discern what God was saying to us.

For many this was the first time they had fasted, and though most had prayed often enough before, the very clear focus for prayer (build or add a service) was new. It was a spiritually rich experience. People were consciously paying attention to what they believed God was saying to them and what it meant for the future of the church. During that time, we had many combined prayer sessions, there was a twenty-four-hour prayer chain running and people had a strong sense that God was about to do something.

I still remember the meeting where we gathered to hear what we believed God was saying to us. I chaired it, but entered without the usual clarity I have about how a meeting should run. I felt that this was primarily about listening to people and that somehow, as we spoke together, what God was saying would become clear.

Most wanted to build. They were confident that people would give their financial support and that we could afford it, and they were keen that we not only enlarge the main auditorium for worship services but also add several other meeting rooms. Someone suggested we purchase some of the surrounding houses and demolish them to make sure we could provide adequate parking. In my head I was hearing the cost of the build go up about $20,000 with every second word someone said!

Then the conversation swung to the case for a second service. There were several fears expressed. We already had a morning and an evening congregation, but would a second morning congregation make us feel as though we were part of different churches? And would the church hold together as closely as it had? And would we run two children's programmes, and if so, how would we staff them? And how would we have enough musicians, and if we simply expected those we had to be at both services were we not being unreasonable? ('After all,' as someone said not too diplomatically, 'good though the sermon always is, it isn't *that* good. Who would want to hear it twice?') Naturally there was the inevitable appeal to tradition: 'This church has been going for almost seventy-five years and we've never needed a second morning service before!' And then there was the bluntly honest approach: 'So what time will the second service be? Because I don't want the time of the present service to change. It works perfectly. I get back from church just in time for lunch at noon, and I don't plan to change the practice of a lifetime.' And so it went on.

It seemed clear to me that a new build would get the numbers up, while a second morning service probably wouldn't, and was just about to suggest that, when an older member of the congregation quietly said: 'Well, I'm not sure if I should say this but does anyone else have a sense that God is saying we are supposed to be doing both?'

'Well, that's interesting,' I thought to myself. 'I imagine it will take less than five seconds to blow that one out the water, but I hope we can say it in a non-offensive way. He's a godly man and I don't want to hurt his feelings.'

A woman quickly spoke up. 'That is exactly what I felt God was saying to me. This is not an exercise of pluses and minuses; we were asked to listen for God's voice. I've been trying to do that, and I really think that is exactly what God has been saying.'

With a speed I would not have thought possible (this was a Baptist church where everyone was used to having their say about everything) the mood changed. You could tangibly feel it. One of the elders summed it up: 'It's both, isn't it? Not what I would have thought, but that is what God is saying.'

And both it was. And it was soon obvious why. Even with our wonderfully enlarged facilities, we would never have been able to fit everyone into one morning service. A time of rich blessing followed.

Though I don't have the slightest doubt that God led us to that decision, I quickly realized that it had many implications for me. The first was simply that my leadership skills would have to improve. In its seventy-five-year history the church had always been small. Thinking small was part of its DNA. While it never grew to be a megachurch, it was suddenly a large church, employing multiple staff and having to operate in new ways. Change was the order of the day. I didn't realize how stretching my leadership journey was going to be. But the first step had been the right one. We had spent time carefully listening to God, and when God spoke, we had found the courage to obey. I guess my first leadership lesson was simply that to be a leader you must be willing to be both a stirrer and a saint, someone willing to stir things up a little and champion change, but someone who also stays close to Jesus, who ultimately is the church's true leader.

# Section A

# Spiritual Practices to Form Us

# 1

## Formed by Life

'Hagar, slave of Sarai, where have you come from, and
where are you going?'

*Gen. 16:8*

I originally trained to be a social worker, and while I only worked for
a few years in that capacity (my heart was always set on becoming a
pastor), I remember one gem from my training, a comment that was
made over and over. I can visualize each of my lecturers saying it: 'You
always start where the client is, not where you think they should be,
nor where you would like them to be, but where they actually are.'

I've tried to remember this principle. As we think of the formation
of spiritual leaders, and perhaps as you think about your own formation for spiritual leadership, it helps to ask the question, 'What's
my starting point?'

My lecturers' clarifications need to be restated. It's not where you
think your starting point should be, nor where you would like it to
be; it's where it actually is. How have you been formed by your life up
to this point? You may be carrying baggage from previous disappointments, or perhaps you are a little weighed down by life, or you might
be basking in a recent success – so many possible options. All our
life experiences go into the mix that makes us who we are right now.
Noting and understanding our starting point is the first step to growth.

For each of us, life is made up of twenty-four-hour days. How
we use these twenty-four hours determines if our life will be more,
or less, remarkable. During every life, stuff happens. The range is
vast – there are moments of delight, dread, decisiveness, drama,
desire, dreariness, disappointment, despair, desperation, dismay,

disillusionment, disgust – and that's just a collection of a dozen 'd' words. Many more could be added.

Though life brings a wide array of experiences, often little is learned from them. Time flows along, with opportunities for growth and development unseized, indeed often not even noticed.

This chapter works with the thesis that God is always at work, and that in the final analysis all of life is in some way providential, providing a platform from which we can mature and become more than we would otherwise be. Even the most painful of experiences can prove to be redemptive. Sometimes the greater the pain, the greater the growth.

But we must not be naive. Growth is not automatic. You may have heard about the funeral of the man who died at 93 of whom it was said, 'Although he lived to be 93, he only really lived one year – and that year, over and over again.' While this is a harsh eulogy, we know that it is often true. Some people appear incapable of learning from life and repeat the same errors again and again. They seem to assume that if it didn't work the first ten, twenty or even thirty times, it must surely work on the thirty-first attempt. It seems not to occur to them that another approach might be needed.

Those who are formed for spiritual leadership learn that God teaches us through the various experiences of our life, and that it is therefore wise to pay attention to life and to the lessons it unpacks for us. Note what I didn't say. I didn't say that they never make mistakes or that they have nothing to regret. I simply said that they allow God to teach them through the experiences of life.

There are different ways in which this happens, but one especially fruitful approach is to adopt a narrative frame for understanding and making sense of our life and the direction in which it is heading.

## Narrative approaches to formation

Narrative approaches to formation encourage us to view life as a book being written. Each day adds some extra sentences to the script. Our life is a story with many chapters, some of which are thrust upon us, and others which we more intentionally shape and direct. Noting each chapter and its content alerts us to where we have come from, and often gives a clear sense of how the book is likely to end. If this is all to our liking, then relatively little is required from us. We are essentially content with the direction of our life and there is no compelling reason to change. Often, however, we fail to see the cause and effect between what has gone before, what is happening in the present, and its likely impact on our long-term future. We need to take active steps to ensure that when our life enters its final chapter we do not sing that saddest of all songs, the 'if only' song – where we lament missed opportunities, and bitterly reflect on ways in which life has cheated us and been so much less than we would have liked.

As we try to understand the present page in our life script, it is as well to remember that we are part of a story that began without us and in which we were minor players in the early years.

In trying to understand your life, ask what was happening in both the lives of your parents and their wider community in the five years leading up to your birth. Perhaps you were born into a wealthy, well-educated family at a stable and secure time in history. Your birth might have been carefully planned by your parents, and everything might have gone according to script.

Note the 'perhaps' and the 'mights' in those sentences, because of course the opposite might have been true.

There are other variables worth noting. Are you an only child? Or the eldest, or youngest? How many brothers and sisters do you have, and are they all from the same parents, and . . . well, the list goes on and on. Each answer points to life experiences which are likely to have shaped and formed you.

There are so many things in life which we don't choose.

We don't choose the time or location of our birth; nor do we choose our parents. We had nothing to do with the skill level of the medical practitioners who helped bring us into the world, nor of the diet to which we were initially exposed. Yet each of these things has had a major impact on our life and probably continues to influence us today.

While there are many different aspects to our past, it can be helpful to summarize where we have come from with some basic questions. Here are eight to help you think about key areas of your life.

When you reflect on your past and where it has led you to in the present, do you essentially feel:

- Cheated, privileged or neutral?
- Disappointed, delighted or neutral?
- A failure, a success or neutral?
- Relationally poor, rich or indifferent?
- Academically thin, enriched or in between?
- Financially stressed, content or average?
- In poor health, physically healthy or about where most people your age are?
- Spiritually dry, alive or somewhere else in the range?

Why not plot it on a table, allowing for some nuance by selecting from a range of 1 to 10, where 1 represents extreme unhappiness, and 10 great delight. You are answering the question, 'When I think about my life at present, I rate myself as being . . .'

|  | 1 | 2 | 3 | 4 | 5 | 6 | 7 | 8 | 9 | 10 |  |
|---|---|---|---|---|---|---|---|---|---|---|---|
| Cheated |  |  |  |  |  |  |  |  |  |  | Privileged |
| Disappointed |  |  |  |  |  |  |  |  |  |  | Delighted |
| A failure |  |  |  |  |  |  |  |  |  |  | A success |
| Relationally poor |  |  |  |  |  |  |  |  |  |  | Relationally rich |
| Academically thin |  |  |  |  |  |  |  |  |  |  | Academically enriched |
| Financially stressed |  |  |  |  |  |  |  |  |  |  | Financially content |
| In poor health |  |  |  |  |  |  |  |  |  |  | Physically healthy |
| Spiritually dry |  |  |  |  |  |  |  |  |  |  | Spiritually alive |

Take a careful look at where you have ranked yourself. If most boxes get a score of 7 or more, you are starting from a position of some strength, and are presumably hoping to move from a good position to an even better one. If there are several rankings of 1, 2 or 3, you are starting from a difficult place. You are probably aware of that, but it is as well to formally note it, saying to yourself, 'OK, so I'm starting from further back than I'd like, but at least I know where I'm starting, and I'm going to see what can be done about it.' Facts are friends, and a realistic assessment of our starting point is more helpful than a dismissive but unrealistic declaration that all is well.

Now do the more difficult part of the exercise. Ask yourself why the rating you have given yourself applies. Has it primarily been about decisions which were thrust upon you and over which you had little control, or is it more commonly about the decisions you have made? Even if the answer disappoints you, or discourages you, face it. The road to growth is blocked until we look truth squarely in the face.

That doesn't mean you have to be ruthless with yourself, harshly condemning every poor action you have taken. Understanding why you make poor decisions can set you free to make better ones. For example, perhaps you've had poor role models and have allowed their distorted view of reality to impact you. Perhaps you have been so hurt or so badly let down that you have little self-worth, and consequently have not cared when you have taken destructive paths. You no longer believe you deserve anything better.

In analysing your starting point, remember some biblical affirmations about what it means to be human.

The opening chapter of the Bible affirms that all people are made in the image of God (Gen. 1:26–27). It is a staggering assertion. In some way, each of us represents a little of what God is like to the world, for we bear God's image, reflecting, albeit imperfectly, what God is like. That's a breathtaking truth.

A closely related portrait appears in the Bible's second chapter, where the opening account of creation is elaborated upon. In Genesis 2:7 we are told that when God made the first man, Adam, he did so by forming him from the dust of the earth and then by breathing into him. It's a striking image. What are the constituent parts of the first human? The dust of the earth and the breath of God. What does it mean to be human? It means that we are the dust of the earth and the breath of God.

The first alerts us to our frailty. When all is stripped away, we are but dust – fragile, vulnerable and commonplace. But that is not all that we are. We are also made from the breath of God. We are God-breathed beings, and this gives us a loftiness which is hard to comprehend. We matter, and matter enormously, because nothing less than the breath of God has animated us.

Who am I? I am simultaneously the dust of the earth and the breath of God. Furthermore, I bear the image of the God who breathed life into me.

Pádraig Ó Tuama in his book *In the Shelter* brings a refreshing and hopeful perspective to Christian spirituality.[1] He suggests we learn to say 'Hello to here', and elaborates by telling the story of a remote tribe in Papua New Guinea who have no word for hello, and so greet newcomers with the words 'You are here', to which the expected response is 'Yes I am'. Pause for a while and think how richly suggestive this greeting is, especially when said to the areas where we recorded a 1, 2 or 3 in the table.

'I am disappointed.' 'You are here.' 'Yes I am.' 'Hello to here.'

'I feel cheated.' 'You are here.' 'Yes I am.' 'Hello to here.'

I am here, and that may be a cause for joy, sadness or indifference, but it is where I am. And if it is where I am, and if I must offer everything to God, I offer this to God.

I am here, but perhaps I have been so longing to be somewhere else that I haven't noticed the wonder and joy of here. I might not have fully noticed the richness of the people who are with me here and now. The day may come when they are not here or I am not here, and that may cause me or them great sadness. So, 'Hello to here.' It is not a place to run from, nor a place to scorn. It will not be where I am forever located, so while I am here let me explore in what way God intends it to be a gift to me and to those in my orbit, for all of life is a gift, even though some gifts take decades to spot. Indeed, my current sense of disappointment, or of being cheated or a failure, may mean that I am willing to be open to God in a way I have never previously been.

## Big blocks

While we are created to reflect the image of the God who made us, it is common for there to be significant blocks in the way. They hold us back from being all we were made to be. It helps to identify them, so that we can carefully examine their impact on our life. When understood, what starts as an obstacle can morph into a source of growth and development.

Some are obvious blocks. The death of a parent during our childhood, or the breakdown of our parents' marriage, or our own marriage, or living through a war, or being sexually assaulted, or fighting a life-threatening illness.

Big blocks can leave us anxious and fearful. They can make it difficult to trust. They may leave us wondering how long it will be until the next catastrophe strikes. They spell the death of innocence. We know not only that things *can* go wrong but also that they often do. We know that we are not exempt from the trauma of life.

Big blocks are usually easy to name. They are, after all, big. When you tell your story and you recount what happened, they are the moments when those listening become quiet, look at you with heightened sympathy, and understand more deeply that you too have struggled and suffered.

Sometimes it is only when you tell your story that you realize how deeply you have been impacted by a block of this type. As you speak, you feel your pulse rate quicken, or sense that tears are not far from the surface. You might even find you want to veer away from the story, rationalizing that now is not the time to burden listeners with the heavy weight you carry from your past. These emotions are usually a sign that the blocks were not only big in the past but remain big in the present. The tough thing about big blocks is that they generally take a long time to get over. Sometimes we never do get over them. Rather than wish them away, we need to ask how we will integrate them into our life story, a story that has our own shape and voice attached to it.

Let me say it again. Big blocks do not have to be permanently destructive. They can be the making of us. Would Nelson Mandela have become the leader he was without his twenty-seven years in prison? Likewise, would the apostle Paul have had the pastoral insight he had without the repeated challenges to his apostleship and his frequent periods of imprisonment? Would we ever have heard of Helen Keller if it had not been for the illness that left her deaf and blind when she was only nineteen months old?

It can be helpful to radically simplify issues. If there have been some big blocks in your life, name them, and then ask if their impact has been primarily destructive or constructive for you. If you are still primarily on the deficit side of the ledger, ask what it would take to experience these blocks as life giving. If that seems a bridge too far (and if the question makes you angry, it is), perhaps there are ways to become more reconciled with what has happened so that you reach the point where you can say, 'Though I would never, *never*, have chosen this, it happened – so it happened. Slowly I am learning that life goes on and can be enjoyable and fulfilling despite it. It will always be a song of lament in my life, but it is a lament that is not without hope, nor without some tenderness.'

I have been asked if it is possible to flourish in 'winter', that is, in the most difficult times in life. I now answer, 'Is it possible to flourish without winter?'

I remember a series of pastoral conversations I had with a church member who died about thirty years ago. Though the discussions ended decades back, they left their mark. She had cancer, and after some early optimism that it would be cured she settled down to the slow realization that her desired three score and ten years would be limited to around fifty-seven. Bucket-list dreams changed with each new treatment failure, and in the end morphed into one. She had a very troubled relationship with her three children, probably because of a messy marriage break-up. She wanted to be at peace with each of them before her life ended.

It started in the usual place. She explained how they had been so unfair to her and were being unreasonable and uncaring. The problem was theirs, the heartache hers.

Except that is not at all the way they saw it. And they had more than a few examples to justify their stance. They felt a little trapped, as though their mother's imminent demise was forcing them to overlook wrongs that had etched deep scars in their psyche. They had each decided they would allow the chill between them and her to thaw a little but were neither looking for nor expecting much more. They anticipated a modest funeral with perhaps a tear or two for what had not been, and then assumed they would get on with their lives with their mother permanently deleted and forgotten. But somehow in the excruciatingly hard work that people sometimes do in winter, something changed. It was a deep-down, paradigm-changing reconciliation. It involved seeing things differently and telling their stories within a new frame – one which made room for frailty, foolishness, error and fear. When all the anger and rage lifted, they realized that the divide between hate and love is often astonishingly thin. What they had accepted as hate was profound love that had been deeply wounded.

Reconciliation and death were not far apart, but this was no longer a funeral of shallow grief. In a strange way it was one of deep gratitude – gratitude for winter, and the flourishing that sometimes only takes place in winter. It was gratitude for reframed memories, memories which now empower and bring hope.

Though the above details probably don't match the big blocks in your story, perhaps the underlying principles are relevant. We often have a past that is all too present. Our spiritual growth and leadership journey invites us to honestly admit where we start from, look our big blocks in the face, and explore ways to make them more friend than foe.


## Smaller blocks

Some blocks are smaller and often seem of little consequence. Because they are less obvious, they may be unnoticed and overlooked. It is for that very reason that they can be disproportionately damaging. They shouldn't be, but because it could seem petty to harp on about them, they are often left to slide and remain unchallenged.

What are some common smaller blocks?

Sometimes it is a tone we have adopted. We might come across as being entitled, as someone who should be given extra advantages simply because we are . . . entitled. This usually goes hand in hand with a lack of gratitude, taking others for granted, or conveying a sense that we are not to be questioned or challenged when we make decisions. We simply view ourselves as being above the scrutiny that is applied to others. While in the short term this can be pleasant and takes a lot of pressure off us, in the longer term it is very damaging. People may resent us or fail to give honest feedback. It is often a challenge for leaders, because followers often treat them as though they are special and able to play by a different set of rules from others. There are real perils in that path.

Where does a sense of entitlement come from? Sometimes a privileged background. At other times it is the complete opposite, and people use it to cover a sense of inadequacy or insecurity.

Then there is the block of cynicism. In many circles a cynical attitude is considered witty and clever, even though in reality people who are perpetually cynical suck the joy from life, render spontaneity near impossible, and find it difficult to trust others. As a result they struggle to form genuinely close relationships, for unwittingly they drive others away.

Bubbling away below cynicism is thinly disguised anger. We might adopt the laughing sneer of cynicism because not far beneath the surface we are disappointed, disillusioned or badly hurt. Each of these leads to anger. Because anger is usually viewed as an unacceptable emotion, we allow it to morph into another form, and cynicism can be the result.

Don't misunderstand me. I am not suggesting that the naive are closest to God. We need to be people who are willing to question and probe, and we should be unafraid to name some things as silly and nonsensical. The issue is when cynicism becomes a way of life or when we automatically assume that anyone who is a stranger is wrong (indeed, for a true cynic, even a friend is wrong). It is a problem when distrust is an automatic default and we are no longer able to spot the good and the lovely because we have closed our eyes and heart to the possibility of their existence. If we can never trust, it is unlikely that we will ever be able to trust God.

And then there are bad habits. They are usually solvable, but need to be identified if they are to be rendered ineffective. It can be the habit of eating our food a little too fast, and so eating somewhat too much. Or we could have got used to giving people an answer before we have listened to what they are saying. Or we may fritter away too many hours in front of the TV screen, or check our social media accounts frenetically to see how many likes our latest post has attracted. We might simply talk too much or be a little too quick to make a judgement about something or be disrespectful to people of a different age or culture, or we may pamper ourselves excessively, never challenging our present position, and so never actually growing.[2]

Identify your little blocks, and then set some goals to overcome them. Even as you do this, the temptation will be to believe that they really don't matter much – or that this is just the way you are, so that's that. Such rationalizations are convenient ways to tell ourselves that we don't need to take responsibility for our formation and growth. Don't fall for them. As you parade out your usual excuses for why things are the way they are, think about the wider life story you are writing. If you continue to tolerate a sense of entitlement, or cynicism, or anger, or bad habits, ask what the wider impact on your life story will be. You could find that your refusal to make some minor changes leads to the writing of a script that is much less than it could be.

Having identified little blocks, it's wise to dig a little deeper.

Is what is bubbling away on the surface a sign of a deeper issue that you shouldn't sidestep? All of life has something to teach us. In Matthew 12:36 Jesus comments that we will be judged for every idle word we have spoken. People routinely misunderstand this as implying that Jesus will use our words to trap us and trip us up ('Remember when you said . . .'). But this is not Jesus' goal. He is stating a simple but profound truth. Everything we say, and indeed everything we do, says something about who we are. Nothing is irrelevant, so if we watch out for the little blocks in our life, we will find that they teach us a lot about who we are.

---

**For reflection**

Let's move beyond theory and embark on an exercise. This task will help you to reflect on your life to date and the forces that have shaped you. Ideally it will not be a one-off activity, but rather one you come back to which makes you increasingly mindful of what presently drives you.

In your formation for spiritual leadership, it is helpful to locate your starting point. One way is to reflect on the tapestry of your life. To do this, draw your lifeline, and reflect on its different stages and the factors that have helped shape you into the person you are today. At the end, share your insights with a trusted friend, or someone who can help you to understand your story with greater clarity. While writing it down is helpful, often what we have written strikes us with greater force when we speak it out loud, which is why it is helpful to share it with someone else.

### The task

- Find an A3 sheet of paper, or something comparable. On it draw a line that represents your life – your lifeline. The line can be straight, curved, a circle, or whatever you deem appropriate.
- Using your lifeline, mark key experiences and events in your life with words, pictures, symbols, expressions, colours. It is your choice. Commence the dating five years prior to your birth (that is to say, include the events that were shaping your parents' world).
- On the line include important
  - people
  - places
  - events (births, deaths, marriage(s), tragedies, traumas, celebrations, important achievements, significant experiences, other things you consider important)
  - church affiliations and spiritual markers (conversion, baptism, leadership roles etc.)
  - spiritual high and low points
  - times of significant insight, discovery, development.
- Attempt to give a chapter and title to each major episode or sequence in your life.
- Consider how these experiences have shaped and moulded you into the person you are today. You might reflect on

physical, emotional and spiritual high and low points, times of greatest satisfaction and accomplishment, as well as of failure and setback.

- It is helpful to do the exercise together with someone you know, perhaps your spouse or a close friend. Talk to them about your findings and listen to theirs. If you cannot find someone to do this with, in your mind discuss it with yourself. You could even view it as an act of prayer, consciously bringing each finding to God, and asking God to give you insight into the matters raised. Talk about:
  - the titles of the chapters and episodes in your life
  - how you would describe the movement and flow of your life
  - any themes or patterns that you observe, and any deviation from the normal pattern.

Also share the following:
  - What was the most significant period of your life and why?
  - Who has had the most influence in your lifetime and why?
  - Any special events that have had a particular effect on your life?
  - Name the most negative and positive factors in your life.

- Sometimes, doing an exercise like this can touch on some deep emotions. If so, note them. Spend some time quietly in God's presence. Ask for some insight into God's perspective on the events that have made up your life, and what future chapter God might want to help you write.
- Name the chapter of your life that you are in and note the key things you should be involved in during this chapter. What do you think the next chapter might be? In the light of the next chapter, what should you be doing now?

# 2

# Formed by Community

I rejoiced with those who said to me, 'Let us go to the
house of the LORD.'

*Ps. 122:1*

As we continue to explore the formation of spiritual leaders, it is reasonable to ask, 'Why are spiritual leaders formed?' A natural answer
is, 'For God's glory, and for the life and leadership of the church and
its mission in the world.'

The answer is important. We live in a highly individualistic age.
You might have started reading this book thinking, 'Yes, I do want
to be formed to be a spiritual leader,' but if asked why, perhaps
would reply, 'Because I want to be the best person I can possibly be.'
While there is nothing dramatically wrong with that, it doesn't go
far enough.

In Matthew 16:25 Jesus teaches a profoundly challenging truth –
that whoever wants to save their life will lose it, while those who
are willing to lose their life for the good news of Jesus will save it. It
is a disturbing reminder that if we want everything to be about us,
things will implode and finish badly.

In committing to formation for spiritual leadership, we are committing to a vision that is bigger than our personal agenda. Healthy
leadership is on behalf of others. Spiritual leadership is on behalf of
the church, which is the body of Christ in the world (1 Cor. 12:27).

Because spiritual leaders serve the church, it is natural that they
must be shaped by the mission and life of the church. This is a simple truth, but one which is sometimes missed.

In recent years it has become popular to embrace what is described as 'churchless faith'.[1] Worn out by too many church-related disappointments, many have opted out of church and are attempting to grow a version of the Christian faith that is 'churchless'. It resonates with the individualism of our time. We have become increasingly suspicious of and cynical about institutions, and the church is usually seen to fit into this category. Sometimes this is for a good reason. There have been far too many abuses of leadership for us to be dismissive of these concerns. Some have experienced the church as an impediment to their spiritual growth rather than as an indispensable aid to it. This is tragic and should disturb us deeply.

The problem with churchless faith is that the Bible knows nothing of it; nor would it approve of it. The good news of the gospel is that we are reconciled not only to God but also to one another. This reconciliation is best demonstrated in the new community we have been called to build, the church. It is not that after conversion to Christ you have a relationship with God and I have a relationship with God, and therefore we have something in common. My conversion to God is also a conversion to God's church, just as yours is. We share a new home together, a home where we are truly family. Many years ago Cyprian of Carthage (d. 258 CE), one of the early fathers of the church, wrote: 'He can no longer have God for his Father, who has not the Church for his mother.'[2]

As we participate in the life of the church, we will find that we are being shaped by the experience.

Chapter 1 explored the way in which life is a teacher, and it provided some exercises to help ascertain our current starting point. Our life in the church will also crucially impact the kind of spiritual leader we become. If we are intentionally open to this, the formation is likely to be significantly more influential than if we resist it or view it as being of only incidental importance. In other words, if I take it as a given that the church needs to be an integral part of my spiritual formation, I will be better placed to both receive from and contribute to the ministry it offers.

Let's look a little more systematically at how we are formed by the church.

## Formed by the faith of the church

We are first formed by the faith of the church. While I have a responsibility to try to understand the Christian faith, I do not have to create it, or as theologian Stanley Hauerwas succinctly puts it: 'we don't get to make Christianity up.'[3] This is immensely liberating. In an age which is often infatuated by the new, we have a two-thousand-year-old story which we hold on to. Indeed, its roots go back even thousands of years earlier to the faith of the Hebrews, for Judaism was instrumental in shaping Christianity.

Christian spiritual formation starts when we allow ourselves to be shaped by the contours of the Christian faith.[4] For example, we do not need to agonize over whether we will believe that Jesus was raised from the dead. Two thousand years of church history affirms that this is one of the key foundations on which the Christian faith stands. The challenge is therefore to decide, not if we should believe in the resurrection, but how we should allow the belief in the resurrection to shape our lifestyle, and indeed, the lifestyle of the church. Courage belongs to the people of God, and it is a courage that flows from the fundamental conviction that death is defeated, that forgiveness is possible and that good ultimately triumphs over evil. This is the faith we embrace when we come to Christ, and this is the faith we must be shaped by.

Read some of the words of the Nicene Creed, the most-used creed in Christianity. Formulated at the Council of Nicea in 325 CE and later revised at the Council of Constantinople in 381 CE, the creed opens with the majestic words: 'We believe in one God, the Father, the Almighty, maker of heaven and earth, of all that is, seen and unseen.'

What does it mean to be formed by this faith? Consider some of the affirmations in this creed. God is proclaimed to be one, Father,

Almighty and maker. There is more than enough in each of these descriptors to keep us pondering for decades.

As we are formed by the faith of the church, we abandon the search for other possible gods, for this God is 'one God'. Furthermore, this God is willing to be described as 'Father'. What is more, this one God, who is Father to us, is Almighty. It is almost too much to take in. In a world where we often feel shaped by our powerlessness, the creed announces that we are linked to the One in whom ultimate might resides. This should shape the way we engage in the world. Furthermore, this God is the maker 'of all that is', and therefore presumably has a goal and purpose for all things. Consequently we cannot allow disinterest to characterize our lives, for if we do, we are disinterested in the purposes of the One we are invited to call Father.

Being formed by the faith of the church is one of the earliest stages of spiritual formation, though it is one which is never complete. As our formation continues, we are invited to trust more deeply, and to more actively live in the light of the faith that shapes us.

Not that our formation by the church is a purely one-way process. In some small way as we work out the implications of the teaching of the church in our life and setting, we contribute towards the shape of this faith. It is perhaps this that Paul is getting at in Ephesians 3:18 when he prays that we 'may have power, together with all the Lord's holy people, to grasp how wide and long and high and deep is the love of Christ'. It is 'together with all the Lord's holy people' that the depth of Christ's love begins to be understood. Put differently, it is in the accumulation of millions and millions of stories of Christ's love that the shape of this love is better understood. Somewhere in those many, many stories is your story – and mine. In this modest way, we help to shape that which is shaping us. Our story has its place, and it matters. It is by no means the only story. But nor is it an inconsequential story. So it is that in losing myself to that which is far greater, I find myself and make my contribution.

**Formed by the fellowship of the church**

It is easy to talk about the church in theoretical terms, but the local church is made up of real flesh-and-blood people. Not that we are likely to forget this if we participate in one. We are soon exposed to the local politics, the doctrinal oddities and the actual history of a particular group of people. It might be an inspiring tale, but then again, it might not.

Today many approach the church as consumers. We look for churches which score highly on criteria that are important to us. For one person it might be contemporary music, short uplifting sermons and a good children's programme; while for another a commitment to social justice, an aesthetically pleasing building and a pipe organ could be the deciding factors. Our greater mobility has seen us move away from the parish concept of church (whereby I attend the church closest to my place of residence) and has allowed other considerations to dominate. Usually we are spoilt for choice, with multiple churches making it clear that they would be pleased to have our support and for us to participate in their programmes. It can make the choice of a church bewildering, and it often leads to muddled priorities.

We might pick the church we attend because we really like the people who attend it. Usually we enjoy the company of people who are similar to us, and who don't challenge our attitudes or thinking. They are comfortable to be around and are often a great support and encouragement in the journey of life. Your family might even go on holiday with other church families, and your children might marry their children.

There is nothing wrong with any of this, except that after a while the church starts to take the shape of a social club. No one challenges our blind spots, usually because they are shared. Church becomes an echo chamber where what we have always believed is repeatedly reinforced. It is both comfortable and reassuring but bears little re-semblance to the church originally founded by Jesus.

The New Testament describes the enormous angst the early church went through in its formation. Much of it relates to the struggle to accept outsiders. Jewish Christians battled to accept the idea that Gentiles were valid converts to the then fledgling Christian faith. They attempted to control their access by insisting that males were circumcised and that Jewish food laws were adhered to.

We should not dismiss this as quaint narrow-mindedness. Feelings ran deep. After all, many of the converts were Romans, and Rome had conquered Israel. While Jesus had taught that we should love our enemies, this was easier in theory than in practice. For many Jewish converts, viewing the enemy as part of the same family of faith was a bridge too far. If they could not ban them from the church, they could at least make sure that entry was as difficult as possible.

Likewise, when slaves were converted it added another dimension to the life of the church. Slaves were usually uneducated and seemed to have little to offer back to the church. The church also needed to act cautiously, in case it was viewed as destabilizing the finely balanced status quo of the time by giving slaves a privilege and standing denied to them in the wider society. Paul's letter to Philemon urges Philemon to accept back his runaway slave Onesimus as a 'brother in the Lord' – radical teaching indeed, that a slave should be viewed as a brother (Phlm. 1:16). There was the real risk that the Romans would view it as traitorous.

Even today we struggle to embrace Paul's claim in Galatians 3:28: 'There is neither Jew nor Gentile, neither slave nor free, nor is there male and female, for you are all one in Christ Jesus.' Imagine how much more difficult it was back in Paul's day, in a highly stratified society where those who challenged the standards of the time did so only by putting themselves at risk. Regardless of how we might now interpret the crucifixion of Jesus, at the time it was triggered by the threat he was believed to pose to the ruling authorities of his day. Those who didn't accept the party line were always in danger.

Clearly it would have been easier for Christianity to have remained as a sect of Judaism, essentially closed to outsiders, and able to be covered by the same protection offered by Rome to Jews at that time. True, it was an uneasy peace, as the destruction of the Jewish temple by the Romans in 70 CE demonstrated. But if Christianity had been viewed as a local subset of Judaism, it could have avoided over 250 years of persecution. It would also now be extinct.

Jesus' final promise to his disciples prior to his ascension was that they would be his witnesses in Jerusalem, Judea and Samaria, and to the ends of the earth (Acts 1:8). It was a vision of a growing and inclusive church. It was open to the 'other', even though genuine openness to the other is rarely comfortable.

Why does this matter?

Real formation by the fellowship of the church takes place most dramatically when we allow it to be shaped by what New Testament scholar Scot McKnight calls 'a fellowship of differents'.[5] This is not diversity for the sake of diversity, but because without it we cannot grow deeper in our understanding of Christ and his love for us. Without it, our view is too narrow, causing us to miss too much.

What am I saying?

In an age of consumerism, if we are to be formed by the fellowship of the church, we should select the church we attend with care. Rather than the usual approach – 'Love the music and love the people who are just like me' – it might be more useful to look for 'a fellowship of differents' – people who are not just like me, but who are also being shaped by the love and grace of God.

I saw this in practice in a church where I served as pastor towards the end of the apartheid era in South Africa. In those troubled days most South African churches were racially segregated, but this was one of a few exceptions. We celebrated communion together once a month, and at those services we usually adopted the Anglican practice of passing the peace, greeting each person with the words, 'The peace of Christ be with you', and most commonly hearing the reply, 'And also with you'.

I remember one communion Sunday watching this diverse group of people wishing peace to one another. There was the young white

Afrikaans man (I mention colour, nationality and gender because they were the all-consuming identity conferrers at that time). He was in the prime of health, a member of the university's elite first rugby team, and looked as though he was made of solid muscle. He was reaching out his hand to a frail, elderly, so-called 'coloured' woman, her body wracked with the cancer that was soon to take her life, and speaking the words, 'The peace of Christ be with you, Tannie Hessie.'[6] She grasped his hand as firmly as she could, looked him directly in the eye and said warmly back, 'And also with you . . . and also with you.'

Then there was the professor of French at the university, well known for his erudite contributions to many TV panel discussions on culture and the arts. He was alongside a young African man, brain injured in an accident no one could now remember, and he too reached out his hand and said, 'The peace of Christ be with you.' The blessing could not be verbalized back, but the warmth of the returned smile made it clear that it was conferred.

Two women at the service had spoken to me that week about their children.

One had phoned in great excitement and joy. During the week, her daughter had heard that she was to be appointed as head girl of her school for the following year. The school was one of the oldest and most prestigious in the country. It was a high honour indeed, and her mother was understandably delighted.

The other conversation had been somewhat different. The other mother told me her son had been arrested that week for possession of drugs. She had been worried about him for a long time but had never thought it had gone this far. She was absolutely devastated, and desperately concerned about what the future would hold for her boy.

They stood there that morning, with such different experiences of being a parent, and clasped hands and wished each other the peace of Christ.

It is powerful when a fellowship of 'differents' come together. We don't have easy answers for one another, nor are we likely to ever understand why life can take such varied pathways, but we can be there for one another, recognizing the simultaneous truth that Paul announces in Galatians 6 that we are to 'carry each other's burdens' (v. 2) even while we remember that each one 'should carry their own load' (v. 5). This is not a contradiction. We do carry our own load, but it is so much more bearable when it is done in a community of support, encouragement and love. In a real way, the backing of the community carries us.

Paul captures this well in Romans 12:15 where we are told to 'rejoice with those who rejoice; mourn with those who mourn'. Church life should never be cold and distant. It is about real life, lived and shared together with gentle hope and tangible acts of kindness. It requires us to be open to one another, to let our barriers drop. Naturally someone must take some initiative to make this a reality. If we are committed to being formed as spiritual leaders, there is no reason why that someone should not be us . . .

It seems fitting to include a word here about the relationship between our spiritual formation and our formation as leaders. If we view them as distinctly different categories, we will trip ourselves up in areas like this. Let me clarify.

Much church growth theory revolves around the notion that homogeneous groups grow fastest. Noting that people feel most comfortable in groups with a similar ethnic, educational, financial, social and linguistic background, the early champion of the church growth movement, Donald McGavran, proposed what is now usually called the 'homogeneous unit' principle. Simply stated, it suggests that if we want a church to grow we should keep it homogeneous – a place where most attendees share significant characteristics, or as McGavran puts it in his seminal work on the topic: 'people become Christian fastest when least change of race or clan is involved.'[7] In a later work he noted that people 'prefer to join churches whose members look, talk and act like themselves'.[8]

While this is likely to be true, we need to question the depth of spiritual formation that takes place in homogeneous communities.

They are usually a little too comfortable to foster the kind of change that characterizes genuine spiritual formation.

It is here that our commitment to both spiritual formation and leadership faces a real tension. Church leaders (and indeed most leaders) tend to be pragmatic. They cast an inspiring vision, but also keep an eye on attendance, financial giving and the comfort level of those in their congregation. Too much challenge, and those indicators usually move into negative territory. If we want our churches to grow, we should keep them homogeneous. The trouble is that when we do this, we end up with a church that looks rather like the church we have birthed today: comfortable, smug and not unlike the local tennis club.

A deeper level of leadership is therefore required, one which sees beyond the short-term gain of adopting a 'whatever works' approach, and which reflects more deeply on the nature of the church, and of the witness of the church in the world. The more difficult route of genuine openness to the other is, in the long term, more fruitful because it gives birth to a church able to offer more than predictable suburbia. Uncomfortable though this process often is, it sees the formation of genuine disciples of Jesus, and in the end this matters more.

The tension between spiritual formation and leadership is therefore only superficial. We need to ask what kind of leader we want to be: one who adopts the quick fix, or one who is confident of being able to look future generations in the eye and say, 'We did the right thing.'

### Formed by the rhythm of the church

When being formed by the faith and fellowship of the church, we soon note the gentle but persistent rhythm of the church year. In its own way it has a significant role to play in our spiritual formation.

The church year is preceded by the church's understanding of what constitutes a day and of the church week.

Genesis chapter 1 portrays six dramatic days of creation followed by a day of rest. After each creative day, a comparable refrain appears. Listen to it: 'And there was evening, and there was morning – the first day' (v. 5); 'And there was evening, and there was morning – the second day' (v. 8); 'And there was evening, and there was morning – the third day' (v. 13), and so it goes on.

There was evening, and there was morning. The order is a little surprising. Surely it would make more sense to say, 'There was morning, and there was evening', for don't we start our day in the morning and finish it at night as we head for bed and rest from our labour? Not according to this pivotal passage. Its sixfold refrain insists on a sequence of night to day, not day to night.

Does it matter?

It matters enormously, for if our 'day' starts with 'night' it implies that we begin in the place of rest and quiet and then move from this state into action. Night is the time when little can be done. It is the time for conversation and rest. As we sleep, we entrust our well-being to the care and oversight of God – for we are no longer alert and fending for our self. We are dependent on the grace of God to see us through the night. We have done nothing to earn this; we simply receive it as a gift before we embark on the work that follows rest.

This is a gentle reminder about the correct order of things. Though we are surrounded by temptations to be defined by our work and activity, it suggests a different sequence, one in which we matter to God and receive the care of God before we have done anything to earn or justify it. The insight should be part of our spiritual formation and leadership practice. We matter because of who God is, not because of what we are doing. Grace and acceptance is the opening word. The night's rest is given as an opening gift before we have a day's worth of activity to justify it.

This is further strengthened by the order of the church week. While in Judaism six days of work were to be followed by a Sabbath day of rest, the early Christians changed their practice, focusing on Sunday as resurrection day. This was the first day of the week and was observed as a day for worship, rest and renewal. Work then began on the second day of the week, Monday.

Our modern electronic calendars try to mask this truth and insist that we view Monday as the start of the week before we get a reprieve on late Friday and our week 'end' can begin. Historically this is not the way the church year works, and it is the church year that should impact our spiritual formation. Starting our week on Sunday is another reminder that we are shaped by the grace of God. We begin the week with rest and worship. Before we have 'earned' the right to a reprieve from our labour, we are given it. It is another reminder that we matter to God not because of what we do, but because of who God is. God is the God who loves us, because God is love. God's love is not contingent on our close adherence to God's instructions. It is a love which is freely given, and it is a love which liberates if we allow ourselves to be formed by it.

One more comment about the church and its different understanding of time.

The Greeks used two words when they spoke about time. The word *chronos* refers to time as a quantitative concept (concerned with how much time, or the minutes and hours of the day); the other word, *kairos*, is qualitative (referring to a decisive or key moment).

*Chronos* is a limited commodity, for our time on earth eventually runs out. Our daily life tends to be shaped by *chronos*. We wonder how many minutes until dinner, or if we will arrive at the airport with sufficient time to board our flight. If we muddle *chronos*, we might miss the start of the movie or offend our host at a dinner party because the meal was ruined while they waited for our long-overdue arrival. If we are chatting to our lawyer, we need to watch *chronos* very closely because many lawyers charge in six-minute slots and it will cost us a lot more if we say something in eighteen minutes that could have been said just as effectively in six.

*Kairos* moves the idea of time away from how much time something takes to the *value* of what is achieved in that time, and *kairos* reminds us that some moments are more significant than others and can impact the future decisively. Paul uses the word *kairos* in both Ephesians 5:16 and Colossians 4:5 when he speaks of the importance of 'redeeming the time' (KJV, i.e. redeeming the *kairos*). His intent is to remind us to spot the significance of key moments in our life and to make the most of them.

*Kairos* is of enormous importance in spiritual formation. We need to spot the significance of what happens to us, and ensure it has a good outcome in our life. This will not happen accidentally but only if we actively 'redeem' *kairos* moments as they arise. In other words, we effectively 'buy back' (or redeem) significant moments by spotting them as *kairos* moments, given to shape and transform us. A married couple may be bickering with each other, and while the argument may consume much *chronos*, it could lead to a *kairos* moment if a statement made is suddenly understood in a new way and leads to greater openness and empathy for the other. If missed, the *kairos* is squandered and buried in the relentless flow of *chronos*.

A helpful spiritual exercise is to ask, 'How did I spend my *chronos* today, and were there any *kairos* moments in the day? If so, have I responded to them?' Every day is made up of 1,440 minutes of *chronos*, but the number of *kairos* moments cannot be known in advance. As we mature we will spot *kairos* moments more frequently, and will start to realize that God is often speaking to us at times and in ways we did not initially anticipate.

How then does the church year help in our spiritual formation for leadership?

In the first instance, it systematically ensures that we reflect on the big building blocks of the Christian faith. Those who come from a liturgical tradition have the key Christian festivals highlighted during special days and weeks spread through the year. Others follow the church year a little more loosely, but the sequence is essentially the same.

The season of Advent reminds us of the mystery of God's incarnation and the wonder that the Divine comes to earth as a frail, vulnerable, baby thing, born not in a majestic palace but in a modest stable, to peasant parents who are citizens of a conquered nation. This is not a truth that is easily grasped. It is one thing to say it, but another to allow its significance to deeply penetrate. It is why we have a 'season' for Advent, allowing enough *chronos* for our reflection in the hope that this will become a *kairos* season for us – one which changes us decisively.

Advent moves to Easter. Our Easter preparation often involves sacrificing something during Lent, that time when many Christians voluntarily give up some luxuries or expose themselves to hardship. This is done to replicate, in a small way, the suffering of Jesus. We know that our suffering is a mere pinprick in comparison to the agony endured by Christ, but it is a tangible way of observing the suffering that God went through on our behalf.

Lent then moves into the yet sharper focus of Holy Week, with the reminder of the last supper on the Thursday, of crucifixion on the Friday, of abandonment on the Saturday, and of the inexpressible joy of the Sunday, when Jesus' resurrection takes place against all the odds. If we do not linger long enough in the Garden of Gethsemane or stand dejected and bewildered at the cross of the suffering Christ, the impact of the resurrection is likely to be muted, perhaps even lost on us. But if we observe the season, again and again, and carve out a generous block of *chronos* for our reflection, it might become a *kairos* season, after which our lives could literally never be the same again.

Resurrection Sunday moves on to the ascension of Jesus. The one who conquered death will return. Because Jesus has ascended, we can be confident that the dust of the earth has now touched the very throne room of God, for our human concerns are fully understood by the God who has dwelt among us. The ascension creates a pang of longing in our hearts as we look forward to the time when the heavenly city will come down out of heaven to the earth, and we will hear the cry, 'Look! God's dwelling-place is now among the people, and he will dwell with them. They will be his people, and God himself will be with them and be their God' (Rev. 21:3).

Pentecost Sunday is remembered ten days later. This, the celebration of the birth of the church, reminds us of our commission to spread the gospel to each and every nation, and to be witnesses of the good news of Jesus to every people-group on this planet, whatever language they speak. It urges the church to be outwardly tilted, not looking to its own concerns but persistently seeking ways in which it may most helpfully reach those who are outside its orbit. It is the reminder that the church exists for the benefit of its non-members, and is a dramatic invitation to receive the power that comes from the Spirit of God alone.

The remainder of the church year, often described as 'ordinary time', lasts from Pentecost (usually late May) to the start of Advent (four Sundays before Christmas). Not that there is ever anything ordinary about the church year. The story of God's love for the world is too remarkable for that. Ordinary time allows us to reflect on other important aspects of the faith: creation, and our responsibility towards it, the lives of the saints and those who have gone before us, the writing of the Scriptures and all that they teach us . . . and so we could go on.

The value of the church year is in its repetition. Some truths need to be heard repeatedly. Indeed, this is often what spiritual formation is about, as the truth of God's love for us and the world slowly penetrates every aspect of our being. There comes a moment when a tipping point is reached and our living becomes a wholehearted response to the love of God. When we lead from this place, we are likely to become the stirrers and saints the church so badly needs.

---

**For reflection**

1. What is your relationship with the church? Are you formed by its faith and rhythms, or have you developed your own practices? If so, what are they?

2. Is your local church essentially an echo chamber of like-minded people or does it reflect some of the diversity found within the Christian faith? Are you more comfortable in a setting where most people share your views or are you willing to have them challenged? Why?

3. Identify some *kairos* moments in your life. In what way have they shaped you?

4. In what way does the church year shape you? Would you like it to have a greater impact on you? If so, what steps can you take to make that happen?

# 3

# Formed by Scripture and Prayer

Let the word of Christ dwell in you richly.

*Col. 3:16 (KJV)*

Do not be anxious about anything, but in every
situation, by prayer and petition, with thanksgiving,
present your requests to God.

*Phil. 4:6*

If both life and the community of the church are key elements in our
spiritual formation for leadership, so too are the tools which God
has provided for our spiritual growth. In this chapter we explore
Scripture and prayer as two important paths to spiritual formation.
There are others – meditation, submission and worship, to name a
few.[1] Accepting that we can't explore all possible options, Scripture
and prayer seem to me to be the two indispensable guides to discuss.

Naturally you can view the discussion as a purely academic exercise where you gain a deeper understanding of these spiritual resources. However, it will be more helpful to view the chapter as
an invitation to participate in new forms of these ancient but ever
relevant disciplines. Why not accept the invite?

## Formed by Scripture

Hebrews 12:1, drawing from the image of the cloud that led the
people of Israel through the wilderness, informs us that we are surrounded by a great 'cloud of witnesses'. These are people of faith

who have gone before us. Many of their stories are recorded in Scripture, a book filled with 'God turned up' encounters, most often captured in moments of high drama and extreme tension. Each account in the Bible has something to teach us; often it has many things to teach us. We might read passages superficially, having not yet progressed from our childhood readings of the text to more adult reflections on what is written. Indeed, if you have been exposed to Bible stories from an early age (and what a privilege if you have), you may need to rise to the insight that the Bible is essentially an adult book, with challenging and often confronting themes. Do not assume you have exhausted its stories because you are familiar with their broad content.

It is one thing to know the stories and teaching of the Bible; it is another to be formed by its vision and instruction. N.T. Wright has perceptively commented that 'for too long we have read Scripture with nineteenth-century eyes and sixteenth-century questions. It's time to get back to reading with first-century eyes and twenty-first-century questions.'[2] In other words, we need a deep grasp of what the Bible meant to its original readers, and to link that understanding to our awareness of our own time and place, so that we can discern how its teaching works its way out in our significantly different setting.

The jump isn't always huge. It is not hard to understand what Jesus means when he tells us to love our enemies. What *is* hard is to do it. Likewise, it is not difficult to know what Jesus is getting at when he tells us that we must forgive others, but understanding the instruction does not make its implementation easier. The challenge presented by the Bible is more often in the realm of obedience than in the realm of understanding.

We shouldn't be dismissive of the intellectual challenges posed by the Bible. History is littered with examples of a poor understanding of a biblical text leading to a tragic outcome.

Consider the outrageous treatment meted out to Nicolaus Copernicus and Galileo Galilei for teaching that the earth is not the centre of the universe and that it revolves around the sun. Copernicus died shortly after publishing his work, so escaped direct persecution, though his book *On the Revolutions of the Heavenly Bodies*, initially published in 1543, was placed on a list of prohibited books in 1616. Galileo did not fare so well, being placed under house arrest for supporting and developing Copernicus's work. The issue was that Psalm 104:5 says that God has set the earth firmly on its foundations and that it will never be moved. Reading the verse with crass literalism, the church leaders of the day concluded that both Copernicus and Galileo were challenging the very authority of the Bible.

Today we are bemused that the text was ever read so simplistically, and readily affirm that the intent of the verse is to remind us that God is the ultimate holder of the well-being of this planet – and that God's oversight is our deepest source of security.

The Bible itself affirms that 'all Scripture is God-breathed' (2 Tim. 3:16), and we should therefore expect our experiences with its writings to be different from our experiences with other literature, for reading Scripture invites a God encounter. Indeed, as we read the biblical text, we often find a strange shift takes place. We begin as readers usually do, evaluating what we read, wondering if it has any relevance to our life, noting some points as being of special interest, and asking why some pieces of information are offered. To all intents and purposes we stand over the text, deciding what we do or don't agree with. And then the change takes place. True, it does not happen every time we read the Bible, but occasionally we will detect a change in posture. The book that we read starts to read us. It speaks into our life, challenging us deeply, refusing to accept our trite rationalizations and dismissive arguments. It invites us into a new and deeper relationship with God. Instead of us standing over the text, we realize it has floated above us and now looks down on us, asking penetrating questions of us, and inviting us to previously avoided depths of obedience.

Theologians note that the Spirit both inspired the writing of Scripture and continues to illuminate it. The Bible is the Spirit's book. It is the most consistent way through which God continues to speak to us.

It is worth pondering the difference between the Bible's inspiration and its illumination.

As an inspired book, we can trust all that we read in Scripture. God's Spirit has overseen its production. What is recorded is intentionally there – and it contains all that is necessary to inform our faith and understanding of God. We should dive deeply into its pages, asking questions of the text, seeing lines of continuity between one of its authors and another, while probing the apparent discrepancies between some. We should be unafraid to ask questions, for our conviction that this is a Spirit-inspired text gives us a quiet confidence that even the trickiest of questions has an appropriate answer. If we have not yet found it, we should be willing to return to the text again and again until we do. As we search, we will note the progression and development of the biblical narrative, and our theology will be richly informed and shaped by the process.

Ideally we won't read this inspired text alone, but with the awareness that literally billions of readers have gone before. Their readings have taken place over two millennia and in a multitude of cultural settings different from our own, each of which has helped to glean additional insights from its teaching. As we read the Bible with the vast company of saints who have gone before, or who are presently reading it in many varied contexts, our conviction that this is an inspired text is likely to deepen. Could anything less than a God-inspired book have anywhere near this impact? It is hardly likely.

For all the security and confidence that the Bible's inspiration gives to us, it fades in comparison to the transforming moment when this inspired text is illuminated to you or me as individuals. At such times I realize that God's Spirit is speaking directly to me or to my community through its pages. Illumination leaves me in the place of knowing what to do and how to act. The focus shifts from understanding to obedience – and finding the trust and courage to act on what God has shown me.

Don't misunderstand me. I am not advocating an entirely subjective reading of the Bible, as though we can reject its teaching if it does not jump out at us and speak to us at a personal level. My trust in God and my conviction that the Bible is God's authoritative word calls me to obey all that the Bible teaches. I can't read Jesus' instruction to forgive, suppress a yawn, and say: 'Nope, didn't feel anything when I read that. Clearly it doesn't apply to me.' Our obedience to the clear teaching of Scripture should not be contingent on a shiver of excitement running down our spine when we read a particular command.

Having clarified this, let me be equally clear that, as we read this God-gifted book, the Spirit's illumination of Scripture is every bit as important as our belief in its inspiration. Knowing how the teaching of the Bible works out in specific situations is often not easy.

Matthew 10:16 instructs us to be 'as shrewd as snakes and as innocent as doves'. This is a perceptive guiding principle, but in actual situations I need to know where to place the weight. The parent of the drug-addicted child who is asking for a second chance (or a seven hundred and second chance) might feel almost desperate. Is this a moment for tough love – a 'shrewd as snakes' time? Or is this a moment for tenderness – an 'innocent as doves' encounter?

In Luke 14:31 Jesus commends the wise leader who refuses to go into battle without first sitting down and counting the cost, but other passages reassure us that God will provide all our needs. We often need to know which voice is speaking more dominantly in a tangible situation. Both are true, but at times I (or the group I am part of) may be called to levels of trust I have not been able to reach before (perhaps convinced that Paul's promise in Phil. 4:19 is the one God is giving: 'my God will meet all your needs according to the riches of his glory in Christ Jesus'), but at other times it will seem that caution is advocated and we are being told to make no bold plan for tomorrow (Jas 4:13).

A cerebral understanding of the text does not exempt us from the need for spiritual discernment. Reading the Bible requires a simultaneous reading of a text that is both inspired and illuminated.

Often the illumination of the text is best understood in community, for the reading of Scripture should not be a purely private affair. It is best to subject my understanding of what God is saying to me through the text to the insight and wisdom of my fellow travellers, my local church family whose knowledge of and commitment to me should make the process of discernment a little easier.

Perhaps I am running the risk of overcomplicating matters. Some who read this will be saying that what they are really looking for are some simple tools to help them understand the Bible better, and some guidance on how to break it down into digestible-sized chunks so that its teaching can be covered in a reasonable space of time.

Fair enough. There are a multitude of helpful guides available. The only word I would add to the discussion is that 'a little but often' is a useful benchmark. Just as it is better for our health to eat moderately at regular intervals (rather than having indulgent periods of feasting followed by remorseful and lengthy periods of fasting), so too it is wiser to have a daily diet of Scripture. While the occasional lapse is unlikely to prove disastrous, 'a little but often' is a worthy guide. True, there are times when reading an entire book of the Bible at a single sitting can be most helpful, and it can certainly help us to gain a broader perspective on what is being taught. Most often, however, pondering a short section of Scripture each day is fruitful. For a sense of continuity, it is usually best that the passages follow sequentially so that you systematically work through a book at a time. However, don't be in such a hurry to get to the end of the book that you don't journey with it deeply, asking God to help you spot the relevance of what you are reading for the way you live the next twenty-four hours.

At times a passage or verse from the Bible might strike you as being a special word from God for you. Eugene Peterson has written of the significance that Mark 16:6–7 had for his pastoral practice whenever he was meeting others:

> I have acquired the habit of quoting this silently, previous to any visit or any
> encounter. 'He is risen . . . he is going before you into Galilee, there you will

see him as he told you.' Every time I show up I have been anticipated; the risen Christ got there ahead of me. What is he doing? What is he saying? What is going on? I enter a room now not wondering what I am going to do or say, but what the risen Christ has already done, already said.[3]

As we develop a habit of daily Bible reading it is likely that some verses will stand out for us and become trusted friends, helping to shape us into the spiritual leaders God has called us to be. Some verses contain so much that it takes a lifetime to genuinely live in the light of what is promised.

Isaiah 43:1 has had that role in my life. It simply 'jumped out' at me over thirty-five years ago. I had been offered a position which I considered to be very desirable, but which would have seen me move out of paid Christian ministry. The call of that verse is strong and direct: 'Fear not, for I have redeemed you; I have summoned you by name; you are mine' (NIV 1984).

Those who advocate the careful exegesis of the biblical text would validly point out that this verse says nothing directly about my call to Christian ministry. It was a promise to regather the undeserving people of Israel from their captivity in Babylon, and to reassure them that despite their punishment and the difficulty of the situation they were about to face, God still had a future for them.

Does that render my application of this verse to my life invalid and presumptuous? Not at all. God's word is living and continues to speak. Naturally we must take steps to ensure that we are not simply whistling in the dark when we say this, twisting different passages of the Bible so that they fit our personal circumstances and say what we want them to say. Testing our application of the verse with other Christians is one helpful method. We should also ask if the verse helps us to trust God more fully, and to live for God more whole-heartedly, or if it primarily props up a hidden agenda of our own, one which in the longer term will lead us away from God.

To decide this, it helps to be able to quickly summarize some of the key teaching of the Bible. As regards its moral teaching, the

Ten Commandments provide a strong foundation for understanding God's ethical concern for our lives. They can be summarized in a variety of ways, but quickly put, Exodus 20:1–17 instructs us:

1.  To serve no other gods
2.  To have no idols
3.  Not to misuse the Lord's name
4.  To keep the Sabbath
5.  To honour parents
6.  Not to murder
7.  Not to commit adultery
8.  Not to steal
9.  Not to give false testimony against another
10. Not to covet

It is not a difficult framework to remember. We can view it in a slavishly literalistic way, being careful to keep the precise instruction, but Jesus challenges us to adopt a deeper reading of the commandments. To those who quickly proclaim their moral virtue because they have neither murdered anyone nor committed adultery, he probes a little deeper – but have you been angry with someone, or have you lusted after someone? This portion of the Sermon on the Mount (Matt. 5:21–30) makes for challenging reading, and few, if any, can walk away from it feeling vindicated.

While we might reflect on the significance of individual passages of the Bible which seem to have our name written on them, we all need to reflect on the wide ethical implications of the moral vision of the Bible. For example, I haven't murdered anyone, and by and large I am not an angry person – and when I am, the anger passes quickly. I can therefore claim to have fully obeyed Exodus 20:13 and largely met the requirements of Matthew 5:21–22. But before I move on, I am reminded that I live in a world of those who have and those who have not. My decision to hold on to my wealth (relative wealth, to be sure) could have been at the expense of someone who would have benefited (perhaps even had their life spared) if I had been more generous. My struggle to be generous could be impacted by my battle with the final commandment not to covet – for subtly the materialism of the age has got to me, and there is a part of me that consistently cries out for more, and for greater and greater financial security. Thousands of children die of hunger each year not because malicious people set out to slaughter them, but because indifferent people (like me) want more than their fair share.

Take another of the commandments. It might be that while I don't actively tell a dozen untruths about another person (and thus violate the ninth commandment not to give false testimony), I subtly portray them in a less favourable light or fail to say something positive about them because of an inner agenda whereby I think I look better if they are seen to be worse.

I could go on, but I suspect the point is clear. Allowing Scripture to shape and to form me requires me to discern those times when God is speaking to me directly and often very personally through a specific passage, while at the same time I am obedient to, and allow myself to be shaped by, the contours of the teaching I find in the Bible.

## Formed by prayer

Richard Foster has insightfully written: 'To pray is to change. Prayer is the central avenue God uses to transform us. If we are unwilling to change, we will abandon prayer as a noticeable characteristic of our lives.'[4] If Foster is right, and I think he is, prayer will be a central component in our formation for spiritual leadership.

If this is so, we need to ask why we are often reluctant to pray. Foster has already suggested one possibility, which is that we might simply be unwilling to change. There are others.

Many view the future as a static and unchangeable given. Viewing the future as set makes prayer seem little more than window dressing, a prop in a play where everything has already been decided in advance, prayer being introduced for the sake of appearances rather than for its ability to achieve anything. This view is sub-biblical, as James 5:16 makes clear with its claim that 'the prayer of a righteous person is powerful and effective'.

It could be that prayer seems like hard work. We need to learn to pray and are often reluctant to place ourselves in the position of a learner. Having seen Jesus at prayer, the disciples are moved to ask 'Lord, teach us to pray', noting that John the Baptist had taught his disciples how to pray (Luke 11:1). It is not that they have never prayed before, but seeing Jesus at prayer sparks a desire in them to develop a deeper and more meaningful prayer life. They don't view their learner status as a strange or shameful position, but one that can be improved with instruction. We should have a similar attitude. Not that we should expect instant results. The disciples are, at best, amateurs in prayer until the day of Pentecost. Despite Jesus instructing them on how to pray, their subsequent actions and attitudes underline that prayer is not a discipline quickly learned, and that a long journey of learning lies ahead. But it is a journey we should take with optimism and hope. God has instructed us to pray, so our efforts will not be in vain.

When we learn something new, we usually give ourselves permission to fail or, at the very least, to have a few attempts before we expect to succeed. This is a practical insight, and we need to check our behaviour in its light. What new things have you attempted in prayer in the last day, week or month? If nothing, have you perhaps stopped viewing yourself as someone who is learning to pray? If so, why? Is it because your prayer life is already all you desire it to be, or have you forgotten the importance of learning to pray – and that learning will often come about through trial and error?

Appropriately, most of us have been taught to make our prayers provisional, and to submit them to the ultimate will and purpose of God. We therefore often end our prayers with disclaimers such as: 'if it be your will' or 'Lord, we know your will is perfect, so please answer as you see fit' – or something comparable. While the humility displayed by such endings is pleasing, it can mean that we have not adequately listened to God in the act of praying. To end with 'if it be your will' reflects uncertainty as to the will of God. If we are uncertain, such an ending is inevitable, but we should be willing to challenge ourselves on this and to ask if we always must be uncertain, and if we always are uncertain, why this is the case.

Except for his prayer in the Garden of Gethsemane – 'yet not my will, but yours be done' (Luke 22:42) – Jesus models a confident prayer life where what is asked for is assumed to be answered in the affirmative. Such confidence only comes when our requests are preceded by a questioning listening, where we wait on God and ask for God's view on a situation. When an answer is received (and over time we develop a gentle confidence about what is and isn't an answer), we pray with boldness and confidence.

Part of hearing from God can be through developing empathy for the person we are praying for. The Bible often points to the emotion of Jesus which preceded his miracles. For example, Matthew 14:14 and 20:34 record that Jesus was moved with compassion before he healed first the sick and then two blind men. Before we pray about something, it can be helpful to ask God to allow us to feel a little of the weight of the situation. As we feel it, we often gain clearer insight into the purposes of God and can pray with greater assurance and authority.

Richard Foster is again helpful on this, writing: 'if we genuinely love people, we desire for them far more than it is in our power to give, and that will cause us to pray.'[5] Once we genuinely desire the best for others, it is almost impossible not to pray, for so much that we hope for them is beyond our power to deliver . . . but we can pray – and pray with the confidence that prayer changes things. Indeed, an ongoing concern for another person or a particular situation is usually a sign that we are called to pray for it. It is something that God has laid upon us, and we must respond by offering it back to God in prayer.

Not that intercessory prayer should be our main form of prayer. Prayers of praise, and quietly practising the presence of God, are every bit as important, perhaps even more so.

Adele Calhoun wisely notes: 'We all live our lives in the presence of God. In fact, we cannot *not* live our lives in the presence of God.'[6] The issue is therefore not whether God is with us, but whether we are alert to God's presence and are responsive to God's attempts to catch our attention. A sound beginning point for prayer is often to practise the presence of God. In other words, we need to become both sufficiently quiet and observant to spot that God is with us and to tune in to God's presence.

There are specific things we can do to aid us in this. A practice I have found to be helpful is the 'hands down, hands up' exercise. It is simple to do, but as I have led others through it, I have been struck by how often God has spoken.

We begin by sitting in a comfortable position and allowing ourselves to become quiet. This can take a little time, especially if we have come from a taxing day. The 'hands down' part of the exercise consciously recognizes this, for after allowing the worst of the noise in our life to settle, we begin by imagining and visualizing the presence of Jesus with us. This is acting on the faith we have. Jesus has promised to always be with us, so when we visualize his presence we simply assume that he has kept his promise and that he is with us. We not only imagine his presence but also visualize his hands open and underneath our own. We place our hands in a downward-facing position and imagine all the burdens we have been carrying dropping into his hands. This is a prayer of release. It might not be our own burdens we are releasing but could be some of the pain and angst of another. We can pray, 'Lord, you know what [Noah, Megan, Jed] is going through. I take their care and I drop it into your hands, and I ask that you carry it for them.'

It can take a while to release our concerns to God and to leave our burdens in the hands of Jesus, but it helps if we name each care and consciously release it into God's hands.

After a while, we shift the position of our hands. We open them facing upwards and wait to see what God will put in our hands. Sometimes, strange though it may seem, God places back into our hands some of the burdens we have just released. It can be God's way of saying, 'I want you to carry this a little longer.' At other times we are charged with new tasks, or given additional strength, or hear God speaking a simple word of encouragement.

From time to time God may place a particular burden upon us. We may sense that we are being called to a specific task – it might even be a weighty and frightening one. If so, we can be assured that when God calls, God equips.

I'd like to finish this section with the quote that started it: 'To pray is to change.'[7] If you don't want to change, keep away from prayer. But if you are committed to being formed as a spiritual leader, prayer will become a close and transforming companion. And when we pray, we quickly remember that we are never alone.

---

### For reflection

1. Think of a time when you felt God was speaking to you directly through Scripture. What happened? What did you learn from it? If you have never had this experience, are you open to it? What might you need to do for it to take place?
2. Are there any Bible passages that stand out for you? If so, which and why? In what way does the passage continue to instruct you?
3. Do you primarily pray with a sense of expectancy or out of duty? What do you think is the role of each?
4. In what way is your prayer life an act of love for others?
5. Do you agree that 'to pray is to change'? If so, what changes has prayer brought about in your life?

# 4

## Formed by Mindfulness, Reflection and Watchfulness

I will look to see what he will say to me . . .

*Hab. 2:1*

I usually enjoy excellent health, but some months back I succumbed to a minor ailment which required me to be on medication for ten days. The doctor informed me that since a likely side effect was sleepiness, I should take my daily tablet half an hour after I finished my evening meal. Came day four, and about thirty minutes after dinner I stopped and thought, 'Have I taken my medicine?' Answer: I had no idea.

I had a vague recollection that I might have but had been so busy doing one thing after another that I really wasn't sure. I tried to recap my activities and to remember what I had done: sent three emails, replied to a text, exchanged a few quick sentences with family members, answered a phone call, put some of my washing away. But had I also taken my medication? My mind was blank. In the end I came up with a brilliant solution. Given that I had ten tablets, and this was the fourth day, if I had taken the dose, I would have six left. I carefully counted my supply. Six tablets – yes, I had taken it. I still don't remember doing it, but I must have.

Welcome to my overbusy world, one which I suspect you share as well. With something always on the go, it is hard to fully take in all that is happening. And that's the problem. In the flow of life so much is missed. The trouble is that God usually speaks softly. While we don't intend to deafen our ears to God's voice, the noise of our living has the effect of drowning out God's gentle whispers. We are much poorer for it.

If we are to hear from God and to be formed by the guidance received, we should review our expectations. Instead of believing that we will hear from God regardless, perhaps we should recite this mantra: 'I hear from God when I become quiet enough to listen.'

Don't read that too quickly. Take a moment to think about the implications. Say it out loud so that you engage your sense of hearing as well: 'I hear from God when I become quiet enough to listen.'

Perhaps you remember the account of Elijah's encounter with God. Despite the stunning victory over the prophets of Baal recorded in 1 Kings 18, an encounter where Elijah displays dizzy heights of trust and faith, 1 Kings 19 shows a very different Elijah, one who is tired, dejected, discouraged and afraid. He had probably thought that 1 Kings 18 would be the battle to end them all, but 1 Kings 19 starts with the announcement that this is not the case and that Queen Jezebel wants to take Elijah's life. Elijah panics. Stress is cumulative, and this threat turns out to be the proverbial last straw. Elijah is more than depressed. He is suicidal. In 1 Kings 19:4 he pleads with Yahweh to take his life away, and then falls into an exhausted sleep. When he wakes, it is to discover that an angel has baked him bread and provided him with fresh water. While we don't know how it worked, the bread and water were enough to sustain Elijah for a forty-day journey which terminated at Mount Horeb. This was the famous mountain where notable God encounters had so often taken place. Another is about to follow.

In quick succession Elijah is exposed to the forces of a wild wind, a powerful earthquake and a terrifying fire. Was the timing accidental? Hardly likely. God is clearly about to do something dramatic, or so you would think. The biblical text is, however, firmly insistent: God was not to be found in the wind (v. 11), earthquake (v. 11) or fire (v. 12).

It is hard to comprehend. If God was not in these events, how did they take place? A coincidence?

The text shifts our gaze so that we see things differently. Dramatic though these events were, God's voice was only heard afterwards in what verse 12 calls 'a gentle whisper', or perhaps even more accurately, the sound of absolute silence.

The challenging implication is that we might more effectively hear God's voice not in the wind, earthquake or fire, but in the gentle whisper that sometimes follows great activity. That's the first principle to underline. Why not say it again? 'I hear from God when I become quiet enough to listen.'

Reaching a place of inner quiet can be difficult, especially in a world that encourages multitasking and frenetic activity. It is not that we fail to draw the most from the experiences we have, but that after a while we don't even remember we have had them, and they disappear into a fuzzy blur of vague memories rarely thought about or drawn from.

One practice which can help to stem this slide is cultivating mindfulness.

## Formation through mindfulness

At its simplest, mindfulness is the practice of paying attention to what is happening in the present moment. It is about being alert to the now, though alert at a range of levels. The term can mean different things depending on your starting point – a psychologist might mean one thing, a Buddhist priest another, and a Christian monk yet another. There are many areas of overlap, but the focus is a little different.

Let me speak about mindfulness as a practice for Christians who want to use it as part of their spiritual formation for leadership.

Jesus taught that the present moment is important (Matt. 6:25–34). He gently reprimanded those burdened with tomorrow's concerns, pointing out that the birds in the sky are not perpetually anxious about what tomorrow might or might not bring but focus instead on the immediate tasks at hand. He urged us to trust God for our future, while opening ourselves to the challenges of the present. Above all, we are to seek first God's kingdom and righteousness.

At any one moment, our attention is usually focused on either something from our past, something in the present or something in our anticipated future.

Reflect on your thought patterns over the last twenty-four hours. Have they primarily been about something that has happened in the past, and if so, has it been with gratitude, wistful nostalgia, regret, anger, sadness or indifference? You might have been largely concerned with the tasks of the present, with barely a backward look and with little thought as to what the future might be. Equally you might have gone through the motions of doing what must be done in the present, but the real drivers for your activity are your goals and hopes for the future. You long for a day when . . . The dream may already be clearly drawn in your mind.

At the risk of overgeneralizing, some people live largely in the past, others almost exclusively in the present and yet others in anticipation of the future. While there are always some areas of overlap, if forced to say which zone you most live in (past, present, future), which would it be?

The writer of Ecclesiastes 3 reminds us that there is a time and place for everything. There is a place for memory and a place for dreams, but mindfulness highlights the importance of observing the present moment and consciously living in it. Put slightly differently, the purpose of our journey does not have to be our arrival but could be the journey itself. Mindfulness helps us remain alert to what is happening along the way.

Some exercises can help with this.

You could sit down quietly and listen to what your body is doing, or if you will, what your body is 'saying' to you.

Sit in a comfortable and relaxed position and pay attention to your breathing. Is it rapid and shallow, or deep and slow? Note it.

At this point don't try to change it, but simply be observant of it. What does it tell you about your present state? You can scan through different parts of your body. Are they tense or relaxed? You could move your focus from your head downwards, finishing with your toes. Become alert to each part of your body.

You could instead choose to focus on the sounds and sensations of the present moment. Work systematically through your senses: what can you see, hear, smell, taste or touch? The exercise is about noticing what *is*. Pay close attention and enter deeply into the experience.

Another popular mindfulness practice is to eat a raisin, but to do so slowly, noticing each action and sensation along the way. It is not about gobbling down a dozen raisins, but about selecting a single raisin and focusing closely on each part of the experience. Again, working systematically through your senses can help the experience to become more meaningful. As you eat the raisin, what do you see, hear, smell, taste and touch?

If you do these exercises seriously (as opposed to simply thinking about doing them, which might well be the case as you read through this chapter) you are likely to be surprised at how much is going on that you usually miss.

Here is another simple thesis. I'm sure you remember the first: 'I hear from God when I become quiet enough to listen.' The second is: 'To live well, I must notice well.'

Noticing begins when we are alert to what is going on inside us, but it doesn't stop there. Any practice that is purely about the self and self-awareness is ultimately sub-Christian, because the Christian faith invariably points us towards the other, and the needs of their world, while also pointing us to God and the activity of God in each situation. When we become conscious of what is happening in our experience, the knowledge can help us more empathetically observe what is happening in the world of the other. Expressed differently, I can move beyond mindfulness (where I am aware of what is going on in my own self) to watchfulness (where I become alert to the other, the wider world and God's activity). When I am present with my own body, and not hijacked by unconscious fears and agendas, I am free to be truly present with others and with God. This doesn't happen automatically. I need to consciously enter the world of others. It starts by listening – listening not just to the words that the other person is saying, but also to the way they are saying them. Pay attention to volume, pace and tone; to the use of vocabulary; to the things they keep repeating, and those they quickly gloss over. Ask what makes their voice suddenly sound angry, or happy, or sad. Notice the words they do not say (why didn't they mention that?). And then there are the clues provided by body language. Spot the moment when they suddenly fold their arms (why have they become defensive?), or when they shift a little further from you, or avoid your eyes. Why did the topic change when it did? It's a rich experience, and the more you notice, the more appropriate and helpful your response is likely to be.

Some of this processing takes place intuitively. People who have trained their listening skills or who have high emotional intelligence often spot these clues without even realizing it. However, don't assume that you fall into this camp. Even if you do, intentional post-experience reflection can help you become better over the longer term.

Noticing is linked to curiosity. When we are genuinely interested in what is happening to another person, we spot things that enable us to serve them as a neighbour. If we ask no questions about the other, or display no curiosity as to why they are as they are, we should challenge our claim that we care about them – for how can we care if we are disinterested?

### Past, present, future

It is not wrong to think about either the past or the future. While mindfulness invites us to embrace the 'now' of our experience, it is not at the expense of other time zones. If we never reflect on the past, we will never learn from it; nor will we celebrate the many good things that happen along the way, or adequately grieve our disappointments and losses. Likewise, if we neither anticipate the future nor plan for it, we rob ourselves of the joy that comes with expectancy, and at a very practical level may be ill prepared for what lies ahead. In addition, while it is untrue to think that everything depends on us, we do have a role in shaping the future, and careful planning for it can be exciting and liberating. Leaders need to set their face towards the future and think deeply about what it is likely to hold, and how their leadership can help mould the future.

Valuable though reflection on the past and future is, we should see the invitation to mindfulness as a reminder of how easily either the past or the future can dominate our living. Mindfulness is a refusal to be robbed of the reality of the present moment.

### *Enhancing mindfulness*

How then can we enhance our mindfulness? Here are some practical steps.

1. Exercise and develop your attention muscles. We don't often think of attention as a muscle, but in its own way, it is.[1] Push it with some exercise, and it will grow. Feed it with endless distractions, and it will atrophy. A withered attention span will result, with endless things simply being missed. What are some strategies to develop our attention 'muscle'?

First, ask if you need to manage attention or refocus attention. In other words, sometimes we are not paying attention to what we are trying to do because our mind is constantly darting off to another activity it finds more interesting. For example, you might be checking how many likes your latest social media post has, allowing it to distract you from the task at hand. Step one is to identify the distractions, and to make and implement a plan to manage them.

Be clear about where you want to focus your attention – while still noticing what is happening on the outskirts of your task. Own the distractions, in the sense that you note and acknowledge what is happening ('I'm finding it hard not to check my social media because I don't want to focus on this task now') and make a conscious decision about them. Possibly you will even abandon the task at hand ('Actually, I now realize that I really don't want to do this, and there is no compelling reason why I should'), or you might decide to focus on it ('It often takes me a while to get into things, but when I do, I feel a sense of achievement and fulfilment, and I'm not going to allow distractions to rob me of that').

Second, pace yourself. Even though you are developing your attention muscle, like any other muscle it needs to be built up over time. Intentionally break away for short periods. Stretch, walk around, get some fresh air. If it is a task that needs to be completed over a long period of time, make sure there are enough breaks for lighter activities, including some that are simply fun. Remember the Sabbath principle: no one should work for more than six days in a row, no matter how important the task. If it matters, it needs to be done well and will only be done well if the pacing is appropriate.

Third, expand the range of what you notice. One of the most effective ways to do this is to systematically run an experience through the grid of each sense: what did you see, hear, smell, taste and touch? Explore your senses one at a time. Many of us favour either the visual or the vocal and do so at the expense of the others. We therefore miss a great deal. As we develop each sense, our attentiveness muscle grows.

Fourth, develop attention by making use of some intentional exercises. You might well have played the game where random items are placed on a tray and you are given thirty seconds to memorize them. Those who do best usually find a way to spot relationships between the different objects, often clustering them together. There are other versions. Think about a room in your home or workplace. Name the items there. When next in the room, check to see which ones you hadn't noticed. Ask why they escaped your attention.

2. We can adopt the four 'H' approach, where we note how each experience impacts us at the level of our head, heart, hands and the holy. Let me quickly unpack this. Recall a significant recent experience. Systematically remember it through each of your senses. What did you see, hear, smell, taste and touch? Now run it through the four 'H' approach: head, heart, hands and holy.

Under the 'H' as 'head', jot down what you have been thinking and observing. Intellectually, what are the problems or questions that this raises? Is there a new piece of knowledge you must explore more fully, or is there a specific problem you are trying to solve, and if so, can you discover more about it so that you are more likely to find a way forward?

'H' as 'heart' reminds us of the old saying that 'the heart has its reasons that the head knows not'. This is a profound truth. Much in life cannot be sorted at an academic level. We need to listen to our heart. What do we feel about this, and why? While my feelings are my feelings, am I happy to own them, or do I need to note them as an area that might need healing? Alternatively, some feelings might need to be challenged. Perhaps I am indifferent to things which should move and impact me, and I may need to explore why I care so little about them.

'Hands' are self-explanatory. Here we dive into the realm of what we are being challenged to *do*. While we begin by noticing, what we notice often leads to action. Pay attention to these necessary actions and allow them to find their place on the agenda. At the appropriate time, we will do them.

The fourth 'H', 'holy', again reminds us that God often breaks through when we become quiet enough to listen and to notice. What starts as an exercise in attentiveness might lead to a genuine God encounter. As was the case for Elijah, it might only occur after the wind, earthquake and fire in my life subsides, and I hear the voice of gentle silence.

3. Take on board the following practical pointers, given in Shamash Alidina's very accessible book *Mindfulness for Dummies*.[2] Alidina

presents these ten tips for mindful living. I've listed each one, though the commentary is my own:

3.1   **Spend some quiet time every day.** For Christians this should be obvious. In an earlier era it was taken as a given that Christians would have a daily 'quiet time' during which they consciously interacted with God. Perhaps it was pushed a little too hard, and as a result many abandoned the practice as being too legalistic, a chore rather than a spiritually enriching practice. Today psychologists routinely advocate conscious quietening as a practice worth cultivating. Regardless, we need to quieten ourselves each day if we are to notice what is happening inside us, and in those around us.

3.2   **Connect with people.** When we meet people, especially new people, we are often so anxious about what we will say to them that we don't take time to notice them – to look them in the eye and take in what we see, and then to listen to what they say, and to understand it from their point of view. Try to imagine what it is like to be them.

3.3   **Enjoy the beauty of nature.** Most days I go for a walk. There are many parks close to where I live. Their beauty is stunning, and there is so much on the go – the insects, birds and flowers each telling a story. I'm stunned at how many people rush through that same landscape, clearly intent on getting the day's exercise, but doing so with their headphones on and listening to various singers belting out their often angry and cynical songs. They are in nature, but they really aren't.

3.4   **Change your daily routine.** This is a very practical suggestion. Most of us are creatures of habit and do things on autopilot. When we intentionally change our routine, it forces us to pay a little more attention. As we do so, new things come into focus. I have been surprised at the different things I spot by simply walking on the other side of the street. From different angles, you see things you otherwise wouldn't.

3.5 **See the wonder of the present moment.** This is an area I am working on. I'm usually future focused and enjoy thinking about the next thing to work on or what I still want to do. But this moment is now, God's present gift to us.

3.6 **Listen to unpleasant emotions.** Many try to deny these, perhaps because they don't want to heed their warning. Emotions come and go. You are not your emotions. Look at them. Move from judgement to curiosity. In other words, suspend judgement as to whether the emotion is appropriate or not, and ask why it is there. Be curious about why you currently feel as you do. Genuine understanding of our feelings is usually a prerequisite to validly deciding which changes will work for us.

3.7 **Remember that thoughts aren't facts.** Thoughts come and go, and our minds are full of them. Seeing thoughts as simply thoughts (rather than defining facts) can be liberating. When we look at our thoughts, we can more objectively decide if we agree with them or not. For example, you might think, 'I'm useless.' That's a thought, not a fact. Look at it. Probe it. Challenge it. Compare it to what God says about you, and the way in which the Scriptures encourage you to think about yourself.

3.8 **Be grateful every day.** The invitation of the old chorus is to 'count your blessings, name them one by one'. It is also advocated by practitioners of mindfulness. We need to note the things we have to be grateful for. It can be an especially helpful practice if you have a restless, anxious sleeping pattern. Before you go to bed, count your blessings. No, don't count the things you are anxious about (though there are times to do that, in a mindful way, objectively looking at them, remembering that you are not your problems) but take an inventory of the things you are grateful for, and sleep on that.

3.9 **Use technology mindfully.** I was interested to see that although Alidina doesn't specifically cite the Sabbath principle, he does suggest having a weekly technology-free day. Just switch off your phone and ignore it for that day. Perhaps nothing has made mindfulness more difficult than modern technology. We check our phones like addicts, often reaching for them first thing in the morning, every few minutes during the day and last thing at night. It wasn't that long ago that we didn't have them. It's time to ask if we've been taken captive, and to intentionally keep technology in its place so that it serves but does not control us.

3.10 **Breathe and smile.** The mere act of smiling helps us to relax. When we relax, we notice more. Consciously slowing our breathing also helps us to think more clearly and accurately. When we smile, we help others to relax as well. This won't happen unless intentionally done. You could even try it now. Just smile, and now breathe more deeply and more slowly.

Let's finish this chapter with a reminder of the two key takeaways:

• I hear from God when I become quiet enough to listen.
• To live well, I must notice well.

**For reflection**

1. Though it seems a strange question, what didn't you notice during the last week? You will have to stop a while and think carefully before you can answer.
2. Do you tend to focus more on the past, the present or the future? Why?
3. What mindfulness practices have you already adopted? Are there some you are willing to try?

# 5

# Formed by Conflict, Disappointment and Failure

You have taken from me friend and neighbour; the
darkness is my closest friend.

*Ps. 88:18*

At the age of 31 I was appointed principal of a Bible college in
South Africa. Its ministry was significant, and it was a surprising
appointment for someone as young and inexperienced as I was. I
poured myself into its work, determined to make a success of it.
Some things went well, but many didn't. I just didn't have enough
leadership expertise to handle some of the complex issues we faced.
As each new problem arose, I determined that I would work a little
harder and give a little more. But I had two young children (our
third had not yet been born) and a wonderful wife, and each decision to put more into the Bible college meant I had a little less time
for them.

This was highlighted the night my father-in-law died. Aged 80,
he had been admitted for heart surgery. While the procedure was
tricky, the doctors thought it would be successful and prolong his
life for several years. It wasn't a success, and he died a few hours after
coming out of the operating theatre. I got the news while I was in
a Bible college board meeting. Coming back into the room, I continued giving my board report as though nothing had happened.
The board chair, who had also been told, interrupted me and said:
'Brian, you don't need to finish your report. It's OK. We're terribly
sorry to hear what has happened, but now you must go and be with

your wife and family. We'll be OK without you tonight.' I blush as I write this, but the reality is that I hadn't even thought of not seeing the meeting through. I felt it was my duty, no matter what. It didn't occur to me that it was acceptable for my personal life to release me from my usual work duties.

A few months later when I was looking at my 3-year-old daughter sleeping serenely, after another bedtime I had been absent for, it struck me that if I carried on as I was, I would have children I didn't know and a wife I barely spoke to. Much as I enjoyed the challenge of the work I was doing, I realized I had accepted this position at the wrong stage of my life. I started thinking of a way to resign without causing too much tumult. Everyone had assumed I would be in the post for a decade or two, and here I was resigning after less than three years. I spoke to an older and wiser friend about my dilemma. I still remember his reply: 'Yes, people will view it as a failure. And you are not used to failing. But wear your failure like a flag. If you let it, it will be the making of you.'

Wear your failure like a flag. It was strange advice, but over thirty years later I remain impacted by its wisdom. Look your failures squarely in the face, don't run or hide from them, or pretend they don't exist, and they might work out for your good. I resigned, and intentionally became the pastor of a small church. It was a downwardly mobile step, but some of the happiest years in my and my family's life followed. And at a later season of life I became principal of a theological college and was there for seventeen fruitful years. There is a time and a season for everything (Eccl. 3:1–8).

The title of this chapter might come as a surprise. Can we really be formed by conflict, disappointment and failure? For many people, failure feels like the end of the road – the 'I tried, it ended badly, so I will never try again' moment. And indeed the harvest of conflict, disappointment and failure can be deeply destructive, leaving us trapped in bitterness and cynicism, a mere shell of our former self. But it *can* have the opposite effect, and our deepest hurts can lead to inner transformation. In Psalm 88 the psalmist audaciously speaks of darkness being not only our friend, but our closest friend. What might this mean for our formation as spiritual leaders?

## When darkness is our closest friend (Ps. 88:18)

I was chatting recently with a man who surprised me by saying that he and his family had been living in Psalm 88 for a fair while – especially in verse 18b. Naturally I had to look it up. The tone of his comment alerted me to expect something that fell a long way short of cheerful, and my instinct was right.

The psalm is hauntingly sad. While it starts hopefully ('you are the God who saves me', v. 1), it finishes in a very different place, speaking about abandonment, rejection and suffering, before its sobering conclusion that 'darkness is my closest friend'. While many psalms speak of struggle and difficulty, they usually find some kind of resolution before the end. This one does not. Understandably it is not a favourite preaching passage, as most churchgoers prefer more encouraging fare for their Sunday diet. But you can't ignore its sentiments, for they are found both in Scripture and in the lived experience of many people. What are we to make of life when we enter Psalm 88 territory?

Notice I said 'when', not 'if'. This is not a quibble, for most people go through a period in life when Psalm 88 seems to be a close fit. This is even more so for those who are in leadership. Dan Allender has written of the most common challenges faced by leaders, and suggests these include crisis, complexity, betrayal, loneliness and weariness.[1] Feel the weight of the list, especially the pain of betrayal and the isolating sense of loneliness that leaders sometimes experience, especially when they have to make important but difficult decisions.

Psalm 88 insists that we acknowledge those times when joy seems a far distant memory, and the present moment is experienced only as an oppressive weight. It forces us to ask how it can be that some decidedly decent people end up in this place, often because of circumstances completely beyond their control. Think of how many people had their lives turned upside down due to Covid-19. It could be that the decidedly decent person is you.

Let's explore the image. What does it mean to experience darkness as our closest friend?

Perhaps it is that, at times, disappearing into darkness feels better than living in light, which constantly exposes the depth of the problems being faced. Or it could be that darkness means nothingness, and when we are struggling with something that seems insurmountable, disappearing into nothingness might be a tempting preferred option.

Perhaps this is not an image to be explained, but one to be sensed. If darkness is our closest friend, life is at a genuinely desperate point. The exact contours don't have to be spelled out. Our common humanity makes it possible for the image to remain unscripted and yet to be fully understood.

Whatever our interpretation, let's not miss the obvious.

This is a psalm of lament. The 'lament psalms' acknowledge that life often does not run to plan. The psalmist's response is to plead with God, then to complain to God and sometimes to even shake a fist at God. While some might gasp at the boldness of this (how can you challenge God?), in its own way it speaks a word of hope. The psalmist rages at God because of a settled conviction that God exists. If God exists, then hope should never be abandoned. Rather than being the victim of random chance (the only explanation for the atheist), the writer of the lament psalm insists that it is worth struggling with God because, no matter how bewildering God's current silence might seem, God's existence means there is always a flicker of hope. As Psalm 30:5 claims, while weeping may last all night, joy will come with the morning.

What does this mean? If darkness is your closest friend, keep complaining to God. Strange though it seems, this is a form of holding on to faith, for it expresses trust that God does know, does understand, does care and will eventually act. Faith has not been abandoned. This firm belief makes the pain of the present unacceptable and vindicates our complaint. We know that God loves us too much to allow our present angst to continue unabated. And so we plead with God, struggle with God and even shake a fist at God, because the moment we leave God out of the equation we have most truly discarded hope. And then darkness really is our only friend . . .

Is there a point to this struggle? At its best it can lead to resilience, clarified priorities, greater empathy, heightened sensitivity to moments of joy, and a deeper trust in God. These can be fundamental to our leadership, treasures that would never have been available if life had been without care or trouble.

## Discovering your leadership voice
### *A process*

While many people grow through their struggles, growth is not the automatic outcome of difficulty. Some problems see people crushed and unable to move beyond them. It is helpful to note a general life process that undergirds personal growth: the orientation–disorientation–reorientation cycle. I'll again use the Psalms to make some comments about the cycle.[2]

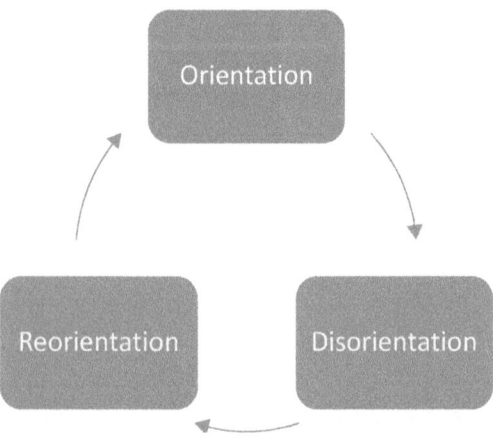

**Orientation.** In the orientation stage we believe that we have largely sorted things out. It is a stage where life makes sense, and we are content with who we are and the setting we are in. We could see Psalm 1 as a classic 'orientation' psalm. Here the psalmist delights in a life which coheres and works. Those who follow God are rewarded; those who do not are like 'chaff that the wind blows away' (v. 4). The summary in verse 6 assumes a world that operates from the cause-and-effect principle, a world which is just and fair:

> For the LORD watches over the way of the righteous,
>> but the way of the wicked leads to destruction.

In the journey of faith, this opening psalm captures the place where most of us begin. It is a stage of happy, optimistic, even naive faith. The pattern laid down in Psalm 1 is most commonly true in life. Usually when we do the right thing, good things flow from it. However, what is usually true is not always true, and when the usual pattern of cause and predictable effect fails to produce the expected outcome, we can be thrown into a state of disorientation. Many factors in life are beyond our control, and when the tide of life turns it can be bewildering.

**Disorientation.** As life progresses, confusing things happen. Sometimes they are devastating. Certainty is replaced by questioning. The book of Psalms may open optimistically, but Psalm 1 gives way to psalms that challenge this view and express confusion, even anger and rage. Psalm 13 opens with the haunting question, 'How long, LORD? Will you forget me for ever?', while Psalm 22 begins in a similar vein:

> My God, my God, why have you forsaken me?
>> Why are you so far from saving me,
>> so far from my cries of anguish?

When we are disoriented, everything seems up for grabs. In the journey of faith, it is a time when some abandon faith.

The stage of disorientation is important because it often sparks a search for deeper and more nuanced answers. It is a time to reject lazy or trite solutions. Sometimes it is the moment when we accept that answers will not be found. It is a stage where we face our limitations, and the limitations of others. Those who embrace the experience of disorientation are often able to empathize with others. From a leadership perspective, only those leaders who have been through disorientation are likely to be safe to follow, as it is very hard for those who have never struggled to understand and correctly 'read' the actions, fears and hurts of others. It is because of this that Henri Nouwen suggests that the best leaders are 'wounded healers'.[3]

**Reorientation.** Ideally, disorientation leads to reorientation. As Psalm 126:5 puts it: 'Those who sow with tears will reap with songs of joy.' The book of Psalms concludes with a series of poems and songs of joyous praise. The individual psalms have trawled the range of human experience, but they conclude that God is good. As the closing verse of the last psalm says: 'Let everything that has breath praise the LORD. Praise the LORD' (Ps. 150:6).

Reorientation does not mean that we live as though nothing troubling has happened. It is a stage where we keep moving in a positive direction even though we have suffered great hurt. It is a time when our pain finds a settled place in our life, where we acknowledge it, but are no longer negatively shaped by or defined by it. It is a part of our story, but it is no longer the only tune we sing.

### A spiral, not a line

The risk in speaking of 'orientation–disorientation–reorientation' is to think that this is a linear journey terminated after it has been travelled once ('Been there, done that, bought the T-shirt!'). It's better to think of it as a spiral. Reorientation quickly settles down to a more complacent orientation. It is not the same starting point as the initial orientation (deep experiences of struggle are not so quickly forgotten), but at some time the new orientation is likely to be unsettled by challenge and turmoil. Life is difficult . . . Personal growth is reflected not in our avoiding times of disorientation, but in facing each period from a starting point that is better grounded. Or, to alter the image, the melody of our life never changes, but we are growing if what started as a tune played with one finger is progressively accompanied by more and more instruments. What was originally dreary and dull develops into music that is majestic and moving.

I've stressed the importance of this process as it reminds us that leadership is neither a point that we reach nor a position that we attain. Both leaders and those who follow them are on a journey. The journey is rarely straightforward. From a Christian perspective, what we become (or are becoming) on the journey is of major significance. Leaders shaped by life's inconsistency are willing to rethink their paradigms and face unsettling truths. They are quietly confident that disorientation will eventually lead to reorientation. Along the way, they discover their own leadership voice.

In his book *The Leadership Ellipse*, Robert Fryling discusses the paradox of the peacock.[4] This most beautiful of birds, so lovely on the outside, has a 'discordant cry'. Put bluntly, it has a horrible voice. Fryling compares this to the dissonance between the inner and outer world of many Christian leaders. Outwardly the appearance might be pleasing, but inwardly our world may be full of turmoil and muddle. Owning our struggles, the orientation–disorientation–reorientation cycle that most of us go through, can be a path to ensure harmony between our inner and outer world.

### Seven key shapers

The chapter title names three difficult things that can become close friends in our spiritual formation for leadership: conflict, disappointment and failure. In fact, I will explore seven close friends (I didn't want the title to get too long), adding four more to the trio of conflict, disappointment and failure: depression, shame, tragedy and false accusation. Before we dive into them, one further insight.

M. Scott Peck starts his classic book, *The Road Less Traveled*, with the observation that life is difficult and that when we are able to accept this, life becomes less difficult. Accepting the normality of difficulty and struggle helps to transform it. Dealing with obstacles and pain is simply part of the price we pay for being alive.[5] Struggle and suffering are great equalizers. Though they comes in different forms and shapes, when we see them as a normal part of life it is a little easier to be compassionate both to ourselves and others, for life is difficult for us all.

Though this might sound like the first of the noble truths of Buddhism (life is suffering), the insight accords with the teaching of Christian theology. We struggle not because we are victims in a villainous world, but because we are humans in a fallen world. From a theological perspective, we live in the 'already and not yet' zone. Christ has come and redeemed us, but we still wait for the new heaven and the new earth envisaged in Revelation chapter 21. Struggle is normal in this in-between time. Rather than being paralysed with self-pity, we should embrace our struggles as a normal part of the embrace of life. Probably there is no greater predictor of the outcome of our difficulties than the attitude with which we face them. If we falsely believe that we are the only ones who struggle, we are likely to feel cheated and angry. If we change the 'Why me?' question into 'Why not me?', it is more likely that a way forward will be found, for resilience is one of the most reliable predictors of success, and is usually possible for those who expect that some periods of life will be difficult, and who are psychologically willing to welcome them as a season for growth rather than as a personal and unfair vendetta against them.

### Conflict

In his Sermon on the Mount Jesus famously proclaims, 'Blessed are the peacemakers, for they will be called children of God' (Matt. 5:9).

People usually like this beatitude. Most of the others are difficult. Let's be honest, the thought of being a mourner or of being meek has very little appeal. But this one is attainable. After all, most people love peace and try to steer away from conflict. So we can at least tick this beatitude box and say, 'Yes, we are peace lovers.' This would be fine if it was what Jesus required, but it isn't. He says, 'Blessed are the peacemakers.' Think about it. There is a very big difference between being a peace lover and a peace*maker*. Peace lovers enjoy the fruit of the work of peacemakers, but the actual peace results from those who make peace, not those who love peace. In short, peace loving is easy, peacemaking is not.

A willingness to face conflict and to deal with it constructively is a key task for those in leadership, and before we think of skills to deal with conflict, we need to consider our own attitude towards it, and ways in which we can work conflict through so that we are peacemakers.

Speed Leas has done some work on the different styles people use to approach conflict.[6] It is helpful to consider these and to identify our preferred style for approaching conflict so that we are aware of both the potential and the pitfalls associated with it. According to Leas, the styles are:

- **Persuasion** – where we primarily use logic and clear arguments to help others to see why we hold the position we do, and, in turn, are most likely to be persuaded to change our own view if the other party logically and convincingly argues their case. If the conflict is about factual matters, this style works well, but if there is an underlying thread of interpersonal conflict based on insecurity, past hurts, prejudice or resentment, it often falls down, because the issue is not about facts but feelings.
- **Compulsion** – where we attempt to overcome disagreement by forcing the other person to do what we wish, often by pointing to our seniority or the positional power we hold over them. In turn, we are most likely to acquiesce because someone holds power over us and uses it to gain our agreement ('Well, unless I wanted to be fired, I had to go along with it; I didn't have any choice').

- **Avoidance or accommodation** – where we don't address the conflict and pretend it doesn't exist, or where we accommodate the wishes of the other party at the expense of our own preferences, rather than face the conflict. While this can work for short-term projects where clear deliverables are required rather than a meaningful working relationship, it usually leads to resentment and breakdown in the longer term. As the poet W.B. Yeats puts it: 'Too long a sacrifice / Can make a stone of the heart' – and there is a limit to how long people can adjust their desires to meet the wishes of someone else.[7]

- **Collaboration** – where we proceed with the assumption that if we continue to work together closely we will find a win-win solution to the vast majority of problems. We approach difficult situations with the conviction that a way forward can be found. Where there is goodwill between the parties, but a practical problem has arisen, this is usually an effective strategy. It is less effective if the other party views the willingness to collaborate as a sign of weakness and tries to take advantage of it.

- **Negotiation** – where we accept that all relationships require some give and take and are willing to give up some of our preferences so long as the other party does the same, and we can reach a solution which we believe to be fair to both. This works best when we can organize our desires and preferences in a hierarchy, so that we are able to differentiate between the things that really matter to us and those that would simply be nice but are not essential.

- **Support** – where we don't really get involved in the conflict situation but rather try to support those who are, helping them to cope with the setbacks and hurts that often arise in conflict situations. This isn't really a style of conflict management, but if it is our preference it helps us identify where we prefer to be in a conflict situation, namely, not in it, but at the side as a support person. While leaders can sometimes play this role, often they must be more directly involved.

While one or two of these styles will appeal to us more, leaders need enough flexibility to adapt their style to suit the situation. Identifying your natural style is a logical starting point, and then developing the skills required for some other styles can deepen what you bring to leadership.

While the focus in this section has been on skills that can help us become peacemakers, don't miss the opportunity for spiritual growth that comes in times of conflict. Conflict often highlights our shadow self. This could be our desire to win at any cost; or our insecurity that feels threatened the moment someone holds a view contrary to our own; or our fear, which makes us avoid telling the truth; or our resentment that someone seems to have brokered a better deal than we did. Dispassionately looking at our response to conflict tells us a great deal. We might not like what we see, but in the end truth is the kindest of friends, and until we face our own brokenness we are unlikely to grow beyond it.

## Disappointment

While some things in life go to plan, many do not. We start with high aspirations and pour many hours into worthy pursuits only to watch them evaporate before our eyes. Disappointment is the usual result. Some disappointments hit us especially hard, and we are left weary, depleted and discouraged. We wonder why we bothered at all, especially if we contributed not just time and money but also our own sense of self.

Some disappointments lead to radical self-doubts. We might question if we have the ability to do what we hoped, or come to the conclusion that we are not as gifted as we thought. Many people have an unconscious Plan A and Plan B for their life. Plan A is what they really long for, but they have a sneaking suspicion they might have to settle for Plan B. If I am an artist, I may dream of a day when the world's leading galleries are clamouring to display my work, but realize that I might have to settle for selling the occasional painting at the Saturday village market. The disappointment may be great.

There is much growth and peace to be found in straddling the gap between Plan A and Plan B. It often starts with a sense of self-condemnation, our inner voice saying: 'As if you were ever good enough for that. Always knew you would amount to nothing.' That voice is usually the toxic aftermath of a multitude of criticisms and put-downs which we have endured over the years. It is at times of disappointment that we discover that those voices have settled inside us, simply waiting for something to go wrong to fire up again and resume their confidence-sapping cry.

Part of spiritual growth is learning to identify this voice and to defuse it. Romans 12:3 advises: 'Do not think of yourself more highly than you ought, but rather think of yourself with sober judgment'. Both parts of this reflection are important. We should not think of ourselves too highly – and when disappointment stares us in the face that is not usually our problem. There is an alternative to an exaggerated sense of self-worth, and that is sober judgement.

Sober judgement moves in two directions. It reminds us that we are not the giant of our dreams, but equally it alerts us to the fact that we are not the dwarf of our fears. Sober judgement is not condemnatory. It objectively looks at our strengths as well as our struggles, and does so in the light of God's love and grace. It is not accidental that Paul continues the discussion in Romans 12 by reminding us that we are members of a larger body and that we belong to one another. My blind spot might be your area of strength, giving you an opportunity to contribute in a way I cannot. And the reverse might well be true. When I view my disappointments in the light of what I both can and cannot give to the body of Christ, I am allowing my disappointments to push me towards maturity and a deeper sense of being part of God's church.

## Failure

I was speaking recently with the key leaders of a group that has successful planted many Christian schools in Australia. While the staff are Christians, over 80% of the many thousands of students who attend these schools do not come from Christian homes. However, large numbers of them go on to embrace the Christian faith because of their very positive schooling experience. At a time when church attendance in Australia is moving steadily downwards, this has been against the flow – a genuinely fruitful mission.

Knowing how successful this school-planting venture has been, and having been involved in a school plant myself, I was keen to know if the group had any secrets of success, for like most people I long to find a 'five-step' solution. The leader of the group looked at me and said, 'You have to be OK with failure. Most people don't realize that two out of three of our school plants fail. They just end up taking large amounts of money, time and emotional energy – and in the end, despite our best efforts, we realize they are not going to work, and we have to go through the painful task of closing things.'

'Are you saying you fail more often than you succeed?' I queried.

'That's right,' he replied, 'but our successes are so significant that in the end they tower over the failures. But if we weren't willing to fail, we wouldn't ever succeed. And when we start out, we are never certain which it is going to be.'

'What do those failures do to your self-confidence?' I asked.

'In the early days they knocked it dramatically,' he replied. 'I would wake up in the night thinking of the people I had disappointed, the money that had been wasted and the sheer embarrassment I was feeling. I would repeatedly ask if we could have known that this would be the outcome and what we could do differently the next time. It was good to agonize like that, because it helped me to identify a few mistakes we made that are now sorted, but it also helped me to realize that for the most part we had acted appropriately in the light of the information available at the time.'

And then he said something that has always stayed with me: 'I realized there was only one test that really mattered. It's what I call the "be comfortable looking at my face in the mirror" test. By that I mean I asked myself if I had acted with integrity, done the best I could at the time, been as kind as I could, and tried to follow what I believed was God's guidance as closely as I could. And I realized that usually the answer was "yes". Though I am far from perfect, even when I failed I had usually done my best, and that was therefore that. I had to leave the results in the hands of God and keep moving along.'

The 'face in the mirror' test. I love it. At the end of the day I have to live with myself, and trust that God knows and understands. It is about building resilience. It is about realizing that not everything finishes in triumph and that how we travel the journey of failure can be even more important than how we travel the journey of success.

But there is an important question begging to be asked.

What happens when we look at our face in the mirror and conclude that we were out of line and that we let the team down badly? Perhaps we didn't pull our weight. Perhaps we weren't as diligent as we should have been in evaluating the information available. Perhaps we were selfish. Perhaps there was a moral failure. In other words, how do we bounce back from failure when deep in our heart we know that we were the key reason (or at least a part of the reason) for the failure?

Truth transforms us for the good, but it can only do so when it is faced. In the end, truth is the kindest of friends, even when its first claim can feel like a devastating body blow.

Truth is a critical part of spiritual formation, for it is an important part of self-awareness. Now it is true that God can help us to be more than we usually are, but this does not alter the fact that God makes us who we are and wants us to be who we are. The best gift we can offer back to God is the best version of our own self, not an artificially contrived one. Put slightly differently, God's gift to us is our life and the natural abilities we are given. Our gift to God is what we then do with them.

When we fail, we should dig deeply into the 'why' question, not to wallow in self-pity, but to more deeply understand what happened. If the answer is that I was playing in a game that did not have my name, I should be ready to make a change. If there are lessons to learn, I must be willing to learn them. If there is forgiveness I need to receive or to offer (for some failures are about other people letting you down), I need to be willing to offer it. I don't finish in the same place that I started, and each failure can be a gift assisting me in my journey of growth.

### *Depression*

While most people suffer from times of sadness and have days when they wake up feeling down, genuine depression is more serious than this. While estimates of the percentage of the population who suffer from clinical depression differ, most fall within the 5–10% range. Genuine depression (as opposed to feeling down) is a medical condition and should be treated as such. Those who suffer from it usually wonder if it excludes them from all but the most minor of leadership roles – especially as the additional stress faced by leaders, plus the long hours leaders commonly work, can trigger fresh bouts of depression. Countering this, many leaders who live with depression find their leadership a lifeline, helping to ensure that they remain engaged with life and providing them with a 'why' to get out of bed each morning.

While I have selected depression, I could have chosen almost any chronic medical condition. Each will pose its own challenge to the leadership potential of those who have it. However, it would be a great mistake to assume that because we suffer from a specific challenging condition it makes leadership impossible. A part of leadership is the ability to inspire others, and often when others see us rising above our own difficulties it motivates and encourages them. Sometimes they actively decide to help us because they see we are committed to a cause despite the obstacles we face. They realize they are needed and can make a difference. Some of the most loyal followers are those who know that without their help, their leader would not be able to continue.

While we should not trivialize any chronic condition which we or anyone else may face, we should allow the Bible to gently push back on our claim that it prevents us from being a leader. Moses claimed that because he was 'slow of speech and tongue' (Exod. 4:10) he should be excluded from leadership – but God saw it differently, and provided Moses' brother, Aaron, for back-up (see e.g. Exod. 4:10–12,30–31; 6:12,30). Paul suffered from an unknown ailment which he described as a 'thorn' in his flesh. His repeated prayers that it be taken away were denied, and replaced with a transforming insight from God, who told Paul simply: 'my power is made perfect in weakness' (2 Cor. 12:7–9). There is something humbling and unsettling about having to lead from weakness, yet in its own way it is remarkably powerful. On the one hand, people respond positively to our courage and vulnerability; on the other, our weakness sees us rely on both others and God a little more quickly. We are not the poorer for it, and we are less likely to fall prey to the arrogance that hinders many leaders, making them blind to the struggles of ordinary people. This is an important advantage.

### Shame

Although once not often spoken about, shame is now a common topic in popular literature. Authors such as Brené Brown have deepened our understanding of shame and helpfully differentiate between shame and guilt, the latter involving 'holding something we've done or failed to do up against our values and feeling psychological discomfort' whereas shame is the 'intensely painful feeling or experience of believing that we are flawed and therefore unworthy of love and belonging'.[8]

Shame is often the product of something done to us, something that makes us feel unworthy and unlovable. It could be as simple as having been ridiculed during childhood for not knowing things we had no reasonable way of knowing, or it might have gone even deeper and involved sexual abuse or some other horrendous evil. Whatever its origin, it leaves us vulnerable and easily exposed, often unable to talk about what has happened for fear of what others might think, or the scorn they might pour upon us. The shame that originates from such experiences is deeply damaging and poisons our experience of life, robbing it of joy, and often leaving us anxious about terrible things that might happen – even though they probably won't.

All leadership journeys start where they start. Most of us have baggage from the past that needs to be dealt with. It can be liberating to realize that what we might experience as our own lonely secret has been the experience of many other people as well. When we put words to our feelings of shame we begin the journey of moving from shame to transparency and courage. Often this journey is best begun with a caring professional counsellor, though sensitive, accepting and insightful friends can make a huge difference as well.

As mentioned above, shame is often the product of something done to us, a time when although we were the victim, we were made to feel like the guilty party. But what are we to do with those times when we *were* the guilty party, and failed to live up to standards which we consider important and hold dear? In reality, it is often even more complicated than that, for categories of villain and victim are not necessarily tidy; villains often started out as victims and now villainize as a result of their pain.

The Christian faith tells a rich story of human dignity and brokenness. In chapter 1 we explored the rich creation account found in Genesis 2:7, which informs us that God made us from the dust of the earth and then breathed into us the breath of life. When asked who we are, we should answer: 'We are the dust of the earth; we are the breath of God.' Both should be spoken thoughtfully. We are but dust – vulnerable, exposed and of little obvious worth. But we are also the breath of God – and that breath gives us infinite worth. The earlier creation account in Genesis 1:27 informs us that we were made in God's image. This is a lofty identity! But it is also a fragile identity, as the repeated failures of humanity recorded in Genesis 3 – 11 amply demonstrate. The world's first parents raise a murderer, for in the biblical story, Cain, the first child born on this planet, goes on to kill his brother, Abel (Gen. 4:1–16). It is not an encouraging start. Much of the biblical narrative is about God's interaction with his rebellious human creation. At the centre of this story stands the cross of Jesus, which offers forgiveness, acceptance and a new beginning.

Being human is complicated. For many it involves a confusing journey with feelings of inadequacy, insecurity and self-doubt. Leaders are not exempt from any of these feelings. Coming to understand them in the light of God's love and forgiveness matters. Flawed but forgiven, when we hold tight to the God who made us, we experience the breath of our Creator flowing into every part of our being, bringing new life, hope, courage and direction.

### Tragedy

In Romans 8:38–39 Paul writes: 'I am convinced that neither death nor life, neither angels nor demons, neither the present nor the future, nor any powers, neither height nor depth, nor anything else in all creation, will be able to separate us from the love of God that is in Christ Jesus our Lord.'

Are these just beautiful words which disappear off the radar when actual tragedy strikes, or do they reflect the experience of believers through the ages? As is usually the case, it depends on whose story you listen to. Undoubtedly there are some whose faith in God has been destroyed by serious tragedy, and if deep tragedy has never struck our own life who are we to judge them?

What I find far more surprising is how often tragedy turns out to be the making of people, seeing them grow in courage, reshaping their priorities, and deepening not only their kindness but also their faith. I have also noticed how often those who hold significant leadership roles have been struck by tragedy. When they speak of it they do not pretend that they were not devastated, but nor do they speak of it as something destructive. It is simply what happened – their story. William Sloan Coffin, during his time at Riverside Church in New York City, compiled a prayer thanking God for 'our more complicated blessings'.[9] It is a rich sentiment, for tragedy can be a 'complicated blessing'.

I would never want to speak tritely about tragedy, and I have seen how devastating it can be. Despite this, as gently, as softly and as tentatively as I can, I try to say to those who stare tragedy in the face: 'Although this is a bewildering and terrible turn in the journey, it doesn't have to be the end. Perhaps you will walk away from it knowing that nothing (yes, nothing) can separate you from the love of God. That knowledge probably won't come today, but if it does, let it transform you.' And I have noticed that it is not only the psalmist who discovers that weeping may stay for the night but rejoicing comes with the morning (Ps. 30:5). Some nights last a lot longer than others, but for many the day of rejoicing does eventually dawn.

### False accusation

Dan Allender, in his book *Leading with a Limp*, suggests that there are five challenges faced by all leaders: crisis, complexity, betrayal, loneliness and weariness.[10] Knowing what to expect can make it a little easier, but only a little. I have chatted through Allender's list in many leadership seminars, and usually ask those present which of the five they find the most confronting. While individuals differ in their answers, almost without exception the group opts for betrayal. Many have a betrayal story to tell, and commonly it's about being falsely accused – sometimes of an action, at other times of a questionable motive, sometimes of hypocrisy or of being a very different kind of person from the person they are. Up to a point most leaders accept this and recognize that when people are disappointed or don't get what they hoped for, they often lash out. Leaders are the easy target. It becomes much more difficult when the person doing the lashing out is a friend, or someone you thought you could trust deeply. But it happens. It happens often.

Exacerbating the problem is that leaders routinely suffer the injustice of silence. Leadership requires us to make tough decisions, and it is not uncommon for them to be made in the light of information that must be kept confidential. For example, a leader might be seen as not caring that a much-loved staff member has resigned and might even be accused of having forced them out because they were jealous of their popularity. But the leader may know that the person has left because they were stealing, or had been involved in sexually inappropriate behaviour, or – well, if you've been in leadership, you are likely to be able to add several more possibilities to the list. Revealing the reason for the departure is often out of the question and would do far too much damage to all concerned, so the leader simply has to smile and carry on when rumours of their callousness circulate back to them.

The 'injustice of silence' can, however, be liberating. Not having to defend ourselves but being content with the 'face in the mirror' test can see us become people of deep integrity. Usually this integrity is recognized over time, and long-standing leaders are often given the benefit of the doubt when confusing decisions are made, though it may cost them some of the relational capital they have built up over time. Those who are newer leaders may be given less leeway, and it can be lonely and painful facing the silent (and sometimes not-so-silent) disapproval of those who have misunderstood the situation.

Having a trusted mentor is invaluable at such times. This usually needs to be someone completely outside the situation who has the benefit of being able to dispassionately assess what has been going on, and who can challenge you if you have been blind to aspects of your own behaviour. Mentors have often been in similar situations and know the injustice of not being able to answer back or provide full information.

Encouraging though mentors are, situations like this provide an opportunity to deepen our trust in God. There is a cost to leadership – why should we assume that we will never have to pay it? It is rather a compliment that God trusts us to remain true even when there is no immediate or obvious benefit that flows back to us.

---

**For reflection**

1. Have you been through a season where darkness was your closest friend? If so, has the season passed? If not, how are you managing the struggle? If it has, what have you taken away from it?
2. Orientation; disorientation; reorientation. Which of these terms most closely characterizes your life now? Why?
3. Which of the seven shapers have most impacted your own spiritual journey: conflict, disappointment, failure, depression, shame, tragedy or false accusation? In what ways have they shaped you?

---

# Section B

# Role Models to Guide Us

# 6

# When Reality Strikes: Some Leadership Studies

We have looked at some helpful principles to deepen our spiritual life and have done so with the awareness that leaders need something extra to help them face the challenges of their calling. But how does it work out in practice?

In the next section I will explore three heroes from the Bible: Moses, Daniel, and Mary. Temperamentally they were not alike, and each faced their near-impossible tasks with a different mindset and a variety of skills. Moses was a reluctant leader; Daniel was a courageous and highly principled leader; Mary was a servant leader who found a way to lead from the second chair. But brief descriptions like this do not do justice to their character or leadership. They were complex people living in stretching times. They didn't always do the right thing, and if they lived in the twenty-first century their underlying leadership ability would have to express itself differently, perhaps very differently! But heroes they were, and there is much we can learn from them.

# 7

# Moses: A Reluctant Leader

But Moses said to God, 'Who am I that I should go to
Pharaoh and bring the Israelites out of Egypt?'

*Exod. 3:11*

## An unexpected start

We are all born into a story that started without us. Moses is no
exception. Search online for 'What year was Moses born?', and a
wide array of answers will be offered. It takes no special genius to
realize that this is not something to be dogmatic about, and that a
reasonably educated guess is around 1500 BCE. Our knowledge of
the history of the time is sketchy, so let's stick to the biblical account
for details of what was going on.

The fortunes of the once-influential Hebrew people have changed.
While their ancestor Joseph had been second only to Pharaoh, this is
a very different time and place, and they are now slaves in Egypt, the
country that Joseph had rescued from famine. A pharaoh 'who did
not know Joseph' had long been in charge and, viewing the Hebrews
as a menacing threat, had subjected them to forced labour (Exod.
1:8). Even that was not enough to calm his fears, so he devised a
plot to have all male Hebrew babies killed at birth. The first version
of his plan was blocked by the courageous resistance of two Hebrew
midwives, Shiphrah and Puah; therefore he turned to version two,
which required the drowning of all male Hebrew babies. Imagine
being a pregnant Hebrew woman at such a time.

For Jochebed this was not an exercise in imagination, but her reality. As her pregnancy progressed, did she pray that the child growing inside her would be a girl? She knew that if not, she would have to throw him into the Nile. Have to throw him into the Nile? Was it 'have to'? The very idea was unthinkable to her, but she knew that the consequence of disobedience could well be her death. Was she one of those people who decided in advance what her decision would be if she heard the words 'It's a boy', or did she decide to face that moment if it arose? The biblical account gives us just a brief glimpse into what was happening for her, for Exodus 2:2b tells us: 'When she saw that he was a fine child, she hid him for three months.' Perhaps she had thought she could obey that terrible command and throw Moses into the Nile, but when she saw the baby her heart rebelled, and she knew that she could not. No matter what the risk was, this was a child she would keep.

Initially it was not too difficult. Presumably Moses was one of those babies who slept well and who slept lots, and the first three months slipped quickly away, with Moses' presence unnoticed by all in authority. But it could not last. Imagine the heartbreak behind the third verse in Exodus 2: 'when she could hide him no longer . . .'

What happened to make her realize that the time had come?

Perhaps Moses had been up all night, wailing loudly, as babies sometimes do. Perhaps her husband Amram had sat her down and told her that they had to face the inevitable. The child could not be hidden forever, the risk they were taking was too great, and they had other family members to think of. Did a furious marital row follow, or was it a time of hopeless and helpless weeping?

We cannot know, but we are told of the plot that was devised. Technically they would obey the pharaoh's order and throw Moses in the Nile, but they would place him in a basket among the reeds so that he would stay afloat. His sister would be watching close by in case the waters of the Nile got too choppy or the baby was in danger of falling out.

To twenty-first-century ears the plan sounds ridiculously dangerous, but Jochebed and Amram had few choices. Realistically it wasn't much of a plan. At best it could last a few weeks. With God, however, the improbable often becomes possible. Sometimes we must embark on a journey only knowing the next step, and this was one of those times. Though Jochebed had lovingly prepared a basket to keep Moses afloat, it is unlikely that she imagined that Pharaoh's daughter (yes, of all people, Pharaoh's daughter) would spot the child, take pity on him and decide she would adopt him. Though I don't doubt that Jochebed prayed for the safety of her baby floating among the reeds, I doubt that she suggested to God not only that he should be found and adopted by Pharaoh's daughter, but also that, as a result of the nimble thinking of his sister Miriam, she, his own mother, would be nominated as the surrogate nurse for the child – and paid to do the job as well. While we often propose to God how our prayers should be answered, this scenario moves well beyond human imagination. But then it didn't depend on human imagination. This was a God-orchestrated event. Though she acted obediently, in the end Jochebed was largely just an onlooker as Yahweh did some extraordinary things. Her boy grows up in a palace, and yet instead of becoming a complacent member of the aristocracy, becomes a liberator of the oppressed. More than this, he receives and delivers God's law to the people he has rescued, a law which in many ways continues to shape our understanding of right and wrong.

According to the law of the time, Moses should have been drowned at birth, but God had other plans.

But God had other plans . . . Those five words say so much. We will learn from Moses the leader, but let's remember that a prior agenda was at work. While we are not mere puppets, dancing in whatever way the puppeteer decides, we are also not completely free. We are born into a story that started without us, and discovering the parts God wants us to play within a much larger plan is one of life's most important tasks. Sometimes we find it by simply putting one foot in front of the other, trusting the good purposes of a loving God.

Scene 1 of the then unnamed baby's life ends on this promising note, the child now a ward of the palace. Exodus 2:10 tells us that he is named not by his parents but by Pharaoh's daughter, who calls him Moses, which sounds like the Hebrew for 'draw out' – a reminder that this child had been drawn out of the water, rescued to help fulfil a plan breathtaking and earth changing in its scope.

### Overplaying your hand

Time goes by. A now adult Moses walks to the site where the Hebrew slaves are working. That walk was to change his life forever. Exodus 2:11 tells us that he spotted an Egyptian beating a Hebrew – realistically not an uncommon sight when there is a master–slave relationship. Why was Moses so thrown by the predictable that he intervened and, in doing so, killed the Egyptian? Not that the act was entirely spontaneous, for verse 12 tells us that Moses had carefully looked around to be sure that no one was watching before he killed and then buried the man.

One suggested answer is that the Egyptian was not simply beating the Hebrew slave, but that he was beating him because the slave had objected that the Egyptian had raped his wife.[1] If so, you can understand that the stakes were higher and that the injustice perpetrated by the Egyptian was all the greater.

We can't be sure, but what is clear is that Moses killed the man and that even his high status as a prince of Egypt did not protect him from the consequences of this killing. When it becomes clear that the Hebrews will not cover Moses' action for him, Moses flees for his life (Exod. 2:13–15). He was to be a fugitive in the desert of Midian for the next forty years.

The incident raises several important issues for leaders to ponder.

Moses probably expected that the Hebrews would be grateful to him for having intervened in this ugly incident. This, however, simply reflects how protected Moses had been in his pampered life in the palace. Moses might have thought that an Egyptian could be killed and buried and that there would be no further consequences, but the Hebrew slaves would not have been so naive. They realized that when the man's death was discovered, the Hebrews would be blamed for his slaughter. Their life was already miserable, but it would be made even worse unless the murderer was identified, for until that time the entire community would have been viewed as suspects and their failure to identify the killer would have been seen as their complicity in the act. Moses had plunged an already vulnerable community into an even deeper crisis.

The leadership lesson must not be missed. A quick emotional response to an obvious evil is not the wisest path to follow. Before rushing to action, we should consider not just how the action might impact us, but also its implication for the community we seek to help. Sometimes the consequences are not what we might initially imagine – as a multitude of well-intentioned but deeply flawed interventions on behalf of vulnerable communities throughout history amply demonstrates. In seeking to help, we may harm. This is a sobering truth that leaders must grapple with.

Naturally this does not mean that we should not help, or that we should turn a blind eye to obvious injustice. But it does remind us that a purely emotional response is not enough. We must care enough to think deeply, and be respectful enough to consult with the people we seek to help. We must not assume that *we* know the answer to the issues faced and *they* do not. Leadership involves looking and listening, and then thinking carefully about what we have seen and heard.

There is another dimension to this account. Though Moses was to lead the Hebrew slaves to freedom, his relationship with them was at best ambivalent. At times they treated him as their liberating hero, at other times as the cause of all their pains and woes. This incident was an early foretaste of what lay ahead. Perhaps it explains his later reluctance to be their leader. Followers are often fickle, and their gratitude can fade. Moses was to experience this, though no one experienced it more than Jesus. Having lauded Jesus for his many miracles, his cheering supporters quickly fled away when the going got tough or his teaching became more challenging. Leadership is a difficult calling, and if pursued primarily for the affirmation received from followers, it is likely to disappoint us. Leaders need a strong moral compass and a deep 'why' that undergirds their actions. Without these, leadership journeys are often abandoned.

## When it all comes to nothing

Moses' flight to the desert probably left him bewildered and bitter. Imagine how he felt when he discovered that Pharaoh knew he had killed an Egyptian and now planned to have him killed. Moses had grown up in the palace and knew that you didn't cross Pharaoh, for if Pharaoh wanted someone dead, their days were numbered. Naturally Moses was afraid and decided that a rapid departure to Midian was the only path to survival.

Life sometimes changes quickly and decisively. The journey from hero to zero is devastating, and for Moses it no doubt led to much angst and self-reproach.

Though very different from life in the palace, his new life was pleasant enough. After impressing the seven daughters of the local priest by heroically driving away shepherds who were preventing them from drawing water for their sheep, Moses goes on to marry one of them, Zipporah, and in time the couple have two sons, Gershom and Eliezer. Moses looks after the flock of his father-in-law, and the years quickly slip away. After much early promise, it looks as though Moses will lead a satisfying but essentially ordinary life.

We can only speculate about what went on inside Moses during this time. Did he have a midlife crisis, losing confidence and direction as he quietly settled into his new life as a shepherd? Did he ever wake in the middle of the night and remember his years in the palace? He must have wondered what those years meant. Most of us have a need to make sense of our life, and we try to see how one chapter in our life story leads to the next. But what do you do when some chapters make no sense? Why grow up in a palace if you are going to spend your adult years as a shepherd? Moses must have sensed that he was destined for more. He probably thought that his impulsive outburst against the Egyptian meant that the plan for his life had fallen apart. Perhaps he believed that he would have to settle for a second- or third-best version of what his life could be.

Although we are speculating, we can say that the Moses who encounters God in a burning bush some forty years later is a very different and less confident Moses compared to the Moses who had rushed to the rescue of the Hebrew slave. The changed Moses is hesitant and unsure of himself. He appears to have accepted that his life was going in no special direction – his early dreams dismissed as fanciful and foolish.

What do you do when your deepest dreams look as though they will never amount to anything? Moses adjusted to a new reality. When God invites him to lead the Hebrews out of Egypt, he no longer wants the job.

## When we don't want the second chance

The Moses who encountered God in the burning bush was not looking for a second chance. Perhaps there had been a day when he had longed for one, and in earlier years he might well have replayed the scene of killing the Egyptian over and over in his mind, perhaps with a persistent lament: 'Why oh why was I so impulsive? Why did I throw everything away?' Maybe, but if so, those days are long gone. But it is not just that those days are gone. He really does not want them back again.

There is a cost to leadership which those who have never experienced leadership often do not appreciate. While leadership does indeed have its perks – influence, recognition and financial gain being just a few – there is another side. Most leaders have encountered public criticism, embarrassment, weariness, loneliness, betrayal and a host of other morale-sapping challenges. Complexity is the norm, and even when things are going well leaders know that a fresh crisis is never far away and will soon be demanding their time and energy.

We do not know the precise day when Moses led his sheep to the far side of the desert, arriving eventually at Mount Horeb, but it is likely that he expected it to be a day much like any other he had experienced over the previous forty years. His expectation would have been far from the reality, for the events recorded in Exodus 3 tell of Moses being given a second chance at leadership, a chance he no longer wants.

In Exodus 3:7–8 God self-introduces as the God who has seen and heard the cries of the Hebrew slaves. Their plight has touched God's heart, and the passage tells of God's concern. It is not a passive concern, for it has led God to 'come down to rescue them from the hand of the Egyptians'. We could summarize the portrait of God painted in these two verses by pulling out the four key ideas: I have seen, I have heard, I am concerned, so I have come.[2]

There is, however, a curious switch in Exodus 3. God does indeed say: I have seen, I have heard, I am concerned, so I have come, but as it turns out, the God who says 'I have come' sends Moses. In other words: I, God, am going to be present through you, Moses. A call to leadership is often the result of a real and obvious need, and this is the case here.

Moses' response to God's call is well known. In many ways it is deeply poignant, as he cries out in verse 11, 'Who am I that I should go to Pharaoh?' A younger Moses would probably have answered that objection by saying, 'I am the one who was miraculously rescued from the Nile and raised in Pharaoh's palace. Who better than me to go?' But that self-assured Moses was destroyed decades earlier. The 80-year-old Moses objects that he is inarticulate and unsuitable for the task. He would have been happy for God to have done the job alone; he is a lot less enchanted by the idea that God requires his participation in it. Moses has become a classic reluctant leader – one of those leaders who lead, not because it satisfies some deep inner longing for recognition or importance, but because they cannot see any other way forward. At the time of God's choosing, God announces a plan to liberate the Hebrews, and Moses finds his name attached to it. God sees, God hears, God is concerned – so we must be involved. It might seem a strange model, but God's concern and commitment to act continues to be the basis of our call to leadership.

While Moses was not enthusiastic about this second chance, we might feel differently. I have met many people who deeply regret mistakes from the past and are convinced that the door to leadership is now forever closed to them. This passage tells a different story. Our journey with God is dynamic and interactive, and fresh opportunities may arise when we least expect them.

## When courage comes

Reluctant though Moses was as a leader, he reached the point of saying 'yes' to God's call. It came after God gave a range of reassurances in response to five clear obstacles that Moses identified.

We looked at the first objection found in Exodus 3:11, 'Who am I that I should go to Pharaoh?' In Exodus 3:12 God speaks the life-giving words, 'I will be with you.' Realistically, this is the game changer. The verse goes on to give Moses a related reassurance, as God informs Moses: 'When you have brought the people out of Egypt, you will worship God on this mountain.' That day did indeed dawn. Sometimes when we are so caught up in the work God has called us to, we don't notice signs along the way that reassure us of God's presence. In advance, God alerts Moses to look for this sign: the day will dawn when the Hebrew slaves have been set free and have arrived at Mount Horeb to worship God. On the one hand, it is obvious that such a day could only dawn if God had performed a miracle. On the other hand, we may get so caught up with the cares of the present day that we forget to step back and remember the extraordinary things that have *already* taken place. God points Moses to future signs, asking that Moses note them and learn from them. For Moses this reassurance is not enough. He raises a second objection in Exodus 3:13, basically saying that he does not know God's name. While he senses that there is continuity between this God who is speaking to him and the God who spoke to his ancestors, Moses still knows very little about the nature and being of this God. God's answer – 'I AM WHO I AM. This is what you are to say to the Israelites: "I AM has sent me to you"' (v. 14) – has intrigued theologians for centuries, but let's not miss the more plaintive plea being issued by Moses. Simply put, Moses is saying to God: 'I don't really know who you are, not even your name.'

This acknowledgement of ignorance is a sound starting point in leadership. While we may think that God selects spiritual giants to be leaders, often it starts differently, with the potential leader having only a fledgling relationship with God, but one which will grow dramatically throughout the journey of leadership. This was to be Moses' experience. In leadership, spiritual growth sometimes occurs as a matter of necessity. There is nothing like being on the front line of action to make you listen more carefully to the voice of God.

Moses raises a third objection in Exodus 4:1, essentially asking what he is to do if no one listens to him or believes him. It is a fair question. Moses had been out of circulation for forty years. Why would anyone pay attention to a shepherd from Midian? God answers by performing miraculous signs in front of Moses. The staff in Moses' hand suddenly morphs into a snake; Moses' hand becomes leprous and then recovers. It is attention-capturing stuff. Moses is assured that God will perform equally startling signs when required.

Moses quickly moves to his fourth objection. In Exodus 4:10 he complains that he is not a gifted communicator and that eloquence eludes him. Note the humour in the passage. Moses is saying that he struggles to speak, but as God is communicating to him through a burning and talking bush, you can almost imagine the bush replying: 'If you find it difficult to speak, what about me?' Clearly God is not limited by our natural ability and provides the strength to overcome the obstacles in our way.

Moses' fifth and final objection gets to the real heart of the matter. In Exodus 4:13 Moses simply says, 'O Lord, please send someone else to do it' (my paraphrase). In other words, when all the excuses are over, a simple raw truth remains: Moses really does not want to accept the mantle of leadership.

In summary, then, these are Moses' five objections to God's call to leadership:

1. Who am I? I don't have the strength to do this (Exod. 3:11)
2. Who are you? God, I don't even know your name (Exod. 3:13)
3. Why will anyone listen? I have no special powers (Exod. 4:1)
4. What about my flaws? I can't even speak clearly (Exod. 4:10)
5. Why not someone else? I really don't want to (Exod. 4:13)

While God is not impressed by Moses' half-hearted response, a compromise is reached. Moses' brother Aaron will be a close second-in-command, and will do the necessary speaking for Moses, although Moses will brief him first about what to say (Exod. 4:14–16). Although not enthusiastic about his call, Moses is now willing to accept it, and begins to make plans for a return to Egypt.

In the end, Moses' reluctance is neither here nor there. The key point is that he responded to God's call. The necessary courage to act as a leader did not come naturally to him, but he reached the point where he laid his objections down and followed God's lead. Many leaders follow a similar path, and if you are a reluctant leader, take heart that you are not the first.

## When followers are fickle

The Hebrew slaves had experienced a terrible time while in captivity in Egypt. There is little doubt about that. Pharaoh had treated them ruthlessly and had exploited their vulnerability. You would imagine that Moses, having liberated them from slavery, would be revered by the people and held in high esteem. But as leaders know, people do not always react in predictable ways. In a remarkably short space of time the liberated Hebrews have reframed their time in Egypt and remember it as a period of happiness and prosperity, a much better life than being pilgrims on the way to a promised land.

Significant journeys are usually fraught with dangers, and theirs is no different. Wandering through desert terrain, they frequently run short of food and water. At other times they face the threat of attack. Their response follows a predictable pattern. A problem arises. The people complain to Moses, blaming him for the difficulty they face, and unfavourably comparing their current situation to the one they had in Egypt. At times the comparison is delusional but is made anyway. Moses then presents the problem to God, usually with some angst. God replies, sometimes requiring Moses to act out some form of response in order for the answer to come (for example, in Exod. 17:5–6 striking a rock at Horeb so that water came out from it). The problem is resolved and the people move on, until the next problem arises and the same cycle is repeated.

Think how draining this process must have been for both Moses and Aaron, for Aaron was usually also drawn in. For example, Exodus 16:3 recounts how the people, before the miraculous provision of manna and quails, complained to Moses and Aaron: 'If only we had died by the LORD's hand in Egypt! There we sat round pots of meat and ate all the food we wanted, but you have brought us out into this desert to starve this entire assembly to death.' Thousands of years after the event, we smile at how ridiculous the complaint was. When had they ever sat around pots of meat in Egypt? But Moses and Aaron were not hearing the complaint thousands of years later. They were hearing it in real time. They were faced with people who were hungry, angry and afraid, and were desperate to find someone to blame for their dilemma.

While leaders sometimes bask in the praise and adulation of those who follow their lead, most know that they should not build their identity on that praise, for it often proves to be transitory and fickle. The strings attached (usually the requirement that nothing is to go wrong) are near impossible to keep in place. When followers lash out, it can be unrealistic and hurtful. Note how emotive the attack on Moses and Aaron was: 'but you have brought us out into this desert to starve this entire assembly to death', as though Moses and Aaron had coerced the people into making the journey and had wanted to see them all starve. At that moment I imagine Moses would have muttered to himself: 'Well, actually, I was never a slave and I wasn't trapped in Egypt. I was living a perfectly contented life as a shepherd in the wilderness – so there has never been anything in this for me. Why did I ever agree to lead such an ungrateful group of people?'

At times the tension rises even higher. Exodus 17 recalls a time when the Israelite community ran out of water. The response of the people is menacing. In verse 4 Moses cries out to God, probably with some fear in his voice, 'What am I to do with these people? They are almost ready to stone me.' In a violent era, it is unlikely that Moses' fear was imaginary. Anger could have turned quickly into violence. While leadership today is less likely to place us in physical danger, we may well be exposed to similar outbursts of anger and rage, and they can leave us shaken, uncertain and emotionally vulnerable.

The relationship between a leader and those who follow their lead can pass through many seasons. While it is often happy and fruitful, Moses' experience reminds us that this cannot be taken for granted. It is a reminder that part of our formation for leadership is likely to require us to handle anger as well as unfair criticism and expectations, without becoming cynical or abandoning those we are called to lead. If Moses found his followers were fickle, we might very well find the same.

## From leadership to leaderships

Like many leaders, Moses did far too much. There is a subtle temptation in leadership to think that no one can do anything as well as you, or to imagine that if you don't do everything, people will not respect your leadership. But leaders who micromanage, and leaders who try to closely control what happens, usually burn out before achieving much.

Exodus 17 and 18 provide an account of Moses' journey to a more inclusive form of leadership.

Exodus 17:8–16 tells the story of Joshua rebutting the Amalekites' attack on the Israelites. While Joshua and the younger Israelite men fight the battle, Moses raises his hands in prayer for them. In verse 11 we read that when Moses' hands were raised in prayer, the Israelites started to win, but when he became tired and lowered them (and spare a thought for Moses – he was in his eighties), the battle turned in favour of the Amalekites. Moses gets progressively wearier as the day moves along, and it seems unlikely that he will be able to stand with upraised arms for much longer. The prospects for the Hebrews seem bleak, until a minor but important strategy shift takes place. Instead of leaving Moses to stand alone, his assistants provide a stone for him to sit on. Furthermore, Aaron and Hur stand on either side of him, each holding up one of his arms. The result is recorded in verses 12b–13: 'his hands remained steady till sunset. So Joshua overcame the Amalekite army with the sword.' What's the bottom line? Joshua could not win the battle without the upraised hands of Moses, and Moses could not keep his hands up without the help of Aaron and Hur.

Who won the battle?

No doubt the Israelites would have quickly and rightly attributed the victory to God. Why else would upraised, praying hands make any difference?

But at another level it was a team effort. Joshua needed Moses' prayers; Moses needed the help of Aaron and Hur. This is a fundamental leadership principle. We need one another. Aaron and Hur took the initiative to ensure that Moses' hands stayed in the air. It was an act of leadership on their part – and the outcome would have been different without it. They recognized that leadership can be enacted at various levels, and that you must move from leadership (singular) to leaderships (plural). This did not mean that the buck did not ultimately stop with Moses (for it did), but that he needed a team of leaders to help fulfil his mission.

This is further reinforced in Exodus 18 when Moses is visited by his father-in-law, Jethro. As parents-in-law often do (I write as one), Jethro watches Moses in action. He is stunned at how busy Moses is. Noting that Moses is acting as the judge for every dispute among the Israelites, he advocates dividing the people into smaller groupings and, as verse 22 says, appointing 'officials over thousands, hundreds, fifties and tens'. A simple principle guided them when choosing whether a dispute was to be decided by an official or brought to Moses, verse 26 summing it up: 'The difficult cases they brought to Moses, but the simple ones they decided themselves.'

Delegation is a lifeline in leadership, and leaders who are unwilling to involve others will almost always frustrate their followers by causing unnecessarily long delays in decision-making. As likely as not, they will also exhaust themselves to the point where, when the genuinely 'difficult cases' arise, they do not have the emotional or intellectual energy left to think the matter through carefully. They might then make a poor decision which could significantly dent their credibility as a leader.

## God in the storm

Though Moses did not know God's name when he was called to leadership, that changed during the journey. As a rule of thumb, the greater the conflict, the closer Moses drew to God. He might have initially approached Pharaoh with a trembling heart and stuttering lips, but the more Pharaoh hardened his heart to what Moses asked, the more confident Moses became. It was as though he spotted the fingerprints of God behind every action, and that was all he needed to keep him moving ahead.

There were times when his encounter with God was overwhelming. I have often heard people talk about a spiritual highlight, but how do you top being called by God to climb Mount Sinai to receive the Ten Commandments and the laws that were to support them? Exodus 34:35 tells us that when Moses returned from his encounters with God, 'his face was radiant'. Over time this would fade, for we cannot domesticate God, but the experiences were rich and real and reflected something of the remarkable relationship Moses had with God.

Despite these dramatic encounters, the lasting impression of Moses' life is that it had long periods of struggle and discouragement. The Israelites were always a mystery to him, for their love for God was at best flickering and fickle. He repeatedly trusted God in the storm. No matter how many miracles took place, they were never enough to convince the Israelites that their next crisis would not prove fatal. Trusting God did not come naturally to them, and that never changed.

This is a reminder to leaders that a life of faith is just that – a life of faith, not of certainty. Some issues never get resolved and must be faced repeatedly. Citing yesterday's provision is often not enough for followers who are panicking about today's emergency. Leaders need to steadily model what trust in God looks like and accept that this is part of their call.

## Muddled endings

Many leaders have a shadow that remains over their leadership and is long remembered. Often the focus is unfair and does not do justice to the strength of their leadership or the contribution they have made. Perhaps this is the way the human mind works. We are wired to remember the scandalous more than the commendable.

Moses does not escape this dynamic. While he leads the Israelites to the promised land, neither he nor his brother Aaron can enter it. It must have been a tough pill for him to swallow, and if his pre-80-year-old life was characterized by regret for killing an Egyptian, the final period would have seen him lament the day he angrily struck a rock to draw water from it, instead of speaking to the rock as God had commanded. The incident is recorded in Numbers 20:1–13, and while biblical scholars continue to debate why Moses was so grievously in error as to deserve this punishment, all accept that something did go badly wrong that sad day. It makes for a muddled ending to the story. Although Moses was undoubtedly a godly man, the ending means we usually add the 'although'.

Perhaps we should not focus on the sadness of this, but rather be a little more philosophical. As leaders, we are chapters, not the entire book. When it is our season, we sometimes think it will last forever. But it doesn't, nor should it. Valuable work usually stands the test of time, and therefore a key test of leadership is the efficient transition from one leader to the next. Moses must be followed by Joshua. Moses had a role to play and it should never be underestimated, but it was far from the complete story. Moses led the Israelites to the promised land. Moses received the Ten Commandments and the laws that expanded on them. This lofty height was achieved despite his deep reluctance to say 'yes' to God's invitation to lead, for we should remember that Moses was a reluctant leader.

Yes, along the way there was the day when the Israelites stopped in the Desert of Zin and stayed at Kadesh. There was no water there, and in a flash of anger Moses struck a rock instead of speaking to it. It appears he thought he could do the miracle unaided and on his own terms. His punishment is that he is not to enter the promised land. This is indeed part of the story of Moses. But the story also tells of the times when Moses' face literally shone because of his close encounter with God. Human leaders are never perfect, and Moses was no exception.

For reluctant leaders, the greatest challenge is to find the courage and discipline to say 'yes' to God's invitation to lead. Moses found that courage. We don't need to add an 'although' to that.

**For reflection**

1. Do you identify with Moses' reluctance to lead? If so, what makes you reluctant?
2. Recollect Moses' five objections to his call, and ask if you ever make similar excuses:
   a. Who am I?
   b. Who are you? God, I don't even know your name.
   c. Why would anyone listen to me?
   d. What about my flaws?
   e. Why not someone else?
3. Are you open to including others in your leadership, and to moving from leadership to leaderships? What might this look like in your setting?
4. What does it take to finish well? What do you do if there is a blot on your record?

# 8

# Daniel: A Principled Leader

Finally these men said, 'We will never find any basis for charges against this man Daniel unless it has something to do with the law of his God.'

*Dan. 6:5*

What image springs to mind when you hear the name 'Daniel'?

If it's the biblical character Daniel you think of, as likely as not you will recall his being thrown into the lions' den for his refusal to stop praying in public. You will remember that the lions did not eat him and that Daniel lived to tell this tale. It is an inspiring story of high principles and great courage and is worthy of its place in almost every Sunday school syllabus. But suggestive though this story is, it only tells part of the account of this remarkable leader, whom I have selected as an example of principled leadership.

It's regrettable that the term 'principled' cannot always be linked to leadership. Many leaders are so driven to succeed that they delude themselves that the end justifies the means. Many compromises lie along this route, and they turn out to be short-sighted. Although some battles are won after moral compromise, what is sacrificed along the way can have a long-term negative impact, for while you might win the immediate battle, it could cost you the war. Leaders who sacrifice the moral high ground for a short-term gain overlook this truth and regret the oversight in the longer term. It is therefore important that we learn from those who have held on to their principles, often at great cost. Of all these leaders, perhaps Daniel has the most to teach us.

We don't choose the era of history into which we are born, or the location of our birth, or the family we are born into, but each impacts us greatly. Daniel is no exception. If you imagine life as a dice rolled against each of these criteria, Daniel scores a 6 for the family into which he is born, for he is part of the nobility of Israel. This is where his good fortune ends, for when the dice rolls for era, he is born around 620 BCE, a time when the superpowers of the age, Babylon and Egypt, are starting to flex their muscles. This would not have mattered if he had been born a Babylonian, but he is not, for he is born in Judah at a time when its people have fallen under the judgement of God and are about to be taken into captivity in Babylon. In short, Daniel is born into a privileged family, but at a challenging time in history and on the wrong side of the military power equation. The odds are stacked against him.

Despite this, his limited advantages turn out to be enough. Daniel's background, added to his age, health, intellect and physical appearance, see him selected to serve in the palace of the king of Babylon. He is likely to have been taken into exile around 605 BCE. Naturally he had no choice in the matter and could easily have allowed the rest of his life to be consumed with rage and bitterness at the loss of his homeland and his exile from his family and relatives.

Tragic though his losses were, the reality is that Daniel lived in a palace and would have been considered highly privileged. It could have been a very different story, for in later raids on Judah the Babylonians became increasingly violent. By 586 BCE, Jerusalem, its temple and all of Judah had been destroyed. Many Jews died, others were taken into exile, and the suffering was immense. Daniel was most fortunate.

## Starting strong

After arriving at the palace, Daniel made his first significant decision. The biblical account is found in Daniel 1. The Babylonians want their talented captives to be fully integrated into Babylonian society and immersed in its culture. Daniel and his three close friends are assigned Babylonian names. Daniel will now be called Belteshazzar (v. 7). When you change your name, it is often a short journey to changing who you are. Daniel has no say in the matter; he is simply now Belteshazzar. With freedom of choice quickly escaping from his grasp, he faced a difficult dilemma. Presented with the fine wines and food from the royal household, Daniel knew that eating this food would involve significant compromise. It had initially been offered to idols (v. 8). His Jewish upbringing and background made him rebel at the thought of eating or drinking it. He considered it defiled. What should he do?

Remember, he was a young man. Food is important at every stage of life, but especially so when you are about 20. He did not struggle with the slowing metabolism or jaded taste buds of old age. This food would have seemed delicious, and no doubt the temptation to accept it was great.

Far and away the easiest option would have been to adapt to the new situation and accept the generous rations provided by the palace. Justifying this decision would have been easy. Flexibility is a key life-skill, and he could also have argued that if the Babylonians had been victorious in battle, perhaps there was nothing wrong with their gods. Though it is unlikely he would have gone this far, he might have fleetingly asked if their gods were more powerful. After all, despite what he had been taught of Yahweh's provision for the Israelites in years past, there was little evidence of it in the present – and you must live in the present. Doubt, hesitancy and ambivalence could easily have characterized this time.

Intuitively, however, Daniel realized how strongly a journey is shaped by its start. Having already accepted a new name, he could easily have accepted a new menu, and with it, an entirely new way of life. In a short time, Jerusalem would have become a distant memory. This is Daniel's 'line in the sand' moment. If he had crossed it, it is unlikely he would have come back again.

He asks the relevant official if he can decline the food. Though not unsympathetic, the official refuses, fearful that he will be blamed if the health of Daniel and his friends declines due to inadequate nutrition (vv. 8–10). Undeterred, Daniel speaks to the guard in charge of him and asks if he and his friends can be allowed to eat and drink nothing but vegetables and water for ten days. He suggests it can be a pragmatic test. If he and his friends look worse than the other young men in the palace, this diet will be abandoned. If they look better, they should be allowed to continue. The guard agrees, and the experiment is successful (vv. 11–16).

While some try to find support from this passage for a vegetarian diet, that probably takes the text further than it wants to go. Verses 9 and 17 both affirm that God was working in the background to make Daniel and his friends successful. What is at stake is not the nature of their diet, but the depth of their commitment. They were determined to find a way to stay true to their faith, and God honours their commitment. They flourish.

Knowing when to yield and when to be unmovable is never easy. At a later point the prophet Jeremiah informed those in exile to 'seek the peace and prosperity of the city to which I have carried you into exile. Pray to the LORD for it, because if it prospers, you too will prosper' (Jer. 29:7). This was a fine balancing act. They needed to be supportive of their new city and yet they could not simply conform to all its standards. The dance involved in being the same as everyone else, yet not quite the same, is exhausting and confusing. Daniel found a way to resonate with the common humanity he shared with others, while he steadily marched to a different tune.

Daniel faced this tension early in his leadership and settled in his mind those things on which he could be flexible and those on which he could not. It stood him in good stead. Daniel is one of only a few biblical characters whose story is told without criticism. He stood his ground early, and he stood it long. He went on to become an outstanding example of principled leadership.

He also shows exemplary self-leadership. As a leader, the first person you lead is yourself. If Daniel had quietly compromised on one principle after another, there would have been no one to call him to account. He was on his own in a foreign land, and the temptation to blend in would have been considerable. A failure to lead yourself can be masked from others in the short term, though in the longer term it becomes more obvious. When we don't prepare adequately for sermons or meetings, or overlook our lax discipline, or start to believe our own excuses, there is often no one to push back. But over time we become a pale shadow of who we could have been. We may never be called to account for this, others simply shrugging their shoulders and concluding that we didn't have as much talent as they initially thought, but in our quieter and more sober moments we will realize that we have let our own self down and that our dreams of what might have been will not be realized. Proverbs 6:10–11 puts it hauntingly:

> A little sleep, a little slumber,
>     a little folding of the hands to rest –
> and poverty will come on you like a thief
>     and scarcity like an armed man.

It might not be poverty that stares us in the face, but simply the sadness of under-achieving, and failing to fully live the one life we are offered.

Daniel does not make this mistake. His self-discipline is outstanding. He clearly realizes that it matters. Let's explore some other key moments in his journey.

## When dreams open doors

Though Daniel and his three friends Hananiah, Mishael and Azariah (to stick to their Hebrew names) impressed all those they encountered, they could easily have been forgotten as a handful of bright-eyed and promising young men who ultimately achieved little. The world is full of people of great promise who don't reach their potential or who find that the right door never opens for them. Daniel's door opens unexpectedly and in circumstances that seem bizarre. The story is told in Daniel 2.

King Nebuchadnezzar has a dream which troubles him and which he wants explained. Perhaps suspicious that his official magicians and sorcerers are a little glib in their interpretations and not to be trusted, Nebuchadnezzar insists that before unpacking the meaning of the dream they must tell him its content. He informs them that if they fail to do so, 'I will have you cut into pieces and your houses turned into piles of rubble' (v. 5). In fairness, while working at the palace had some perks, there was also a significant downside. A despotic king was part of it.

To cut a longish story short, Daniel and his friends are caught up in the controversy, and face being chopped into pieces along with all the other wise men of Babylon. There is nothing like the threat of execution to bring fresh focus to one's prayer life, and Daniel gets his three friends to join him in praying that God will show him both what the king had dreamt and what it meant. God answers their prayer in the affirmative, and Daniel confidently announces to Arioch, the appointed executioner, that his services will no longer be required, for he can interpret the dream. He is taken to King Nebuchadnezzar, and when asked by the king if he can tell him what his dream meant, he gives the memorable reply recorded in verses 27–28: 'No wise man, enchanter, magician or diviner can explain to the king the mystery he has asked about, but there is a God in heaven who reveals mysteries.'

The rest is history.

Daniel recounts the dream and interprets it. Nebuchadnezzar is overwhelmed by what he hears, and though he promotes Daniel to a high position, does not forget that Daniel had attributed his interpretive ability to his God. In words made even more poignant because they come from the lips of a foreign king, Nebuchadnezzar says: 'Surely your God is the God of gods and the Lord of kings and a revealer of mysteries, for you were able to reveal this mystery' (v. 47).

Promoted and now holding significant power, Daniel successfully asks the king to give important positions to his three praying friends, Shadrach, Meshach and Abednego (to now give them their Babylonian names). From a leadership perspective this can be interpreted in either a negative or positive light.

Seen negatively, you could view this as 'jobs for the boys' – in other words, opening doors for your friends so that you never face any robust questions about your leadership, or any serious scrutiny of your actions. Your friends are in your debt and you won't let them forget it – especially if a difficult situation arises. The danger works the other way as well. It is far more difficult to censure an underperforming friend (and perhaps even dismiss them) than someone whose relationship with you is purely professional. There are dangers in promoting those close to you to positions of influence, and leaders should be alert to the risks.

There is another side which we should note. While the king is delighted with Daniel, as a newcomer to Babylon it is likely that his quick catapult to fame would have been met with deep resentment by those who had been there far longer. Though they might have smiled politely in his presence, they viewed him as an enemy and quickly started to plot his downfall. Some contexts are inherently toxic, and you need to have friends in positions of influence who can look out for you. As the story progresses, it becomes clear that Daniel has made the right call on this – though in the short term it is his friends who find themselves in the greatest danger.

Sometimes the risk is different. While Daniel was in physical danger, our challenge might be that current team members hold inherently different values and priorities from the ones we need to implement. At such times, leaders could bring friends and trusted colleagues with similar commitments and values onto the team, so they are not prevented from bringing about needed change by those who have long been in power and who are determined not to budge from the status quo. You might need to consciously work to get allies on your team, in case you don't have enough support to bring about change. Those in leadership quickly realize that a very fine line exists here, and it is important to be aware of it.

## When there is Another in the fire

Though Daniel is not directly caught up in the next conflict, Daniel 3 gives us a deeper appreciation of the complexity of his context.

A common religion can be a unifying force in society, especially if the society is made up of people from different cultural and national backgrounds. Finding a deity who can be worshipped by everyone is a way to provide societal glue, binding otherwise diverse people together. Perhaps this is what Nebuchadnezzar had in mind when he built a 90-foot-high and 9-foot-wide gold-plated idol, probably representing the god Nabu after whom Nebuchadnezzar was named. While a 90-foot-high statue might not sound especially significant to twenty-first-century ears, remember, these were not twenty-first-century ears. This was an impressive engineering feat for the time, and the country would have been wild with pride and admiration at the achievement. All are instructed to bow down and worship this idol when summoned to do so.

Such proclamations were always a nightmare to the Jews, for their faith prohibited them from worshipping any god other than Yahweh. Their choice was stark. Refuse to worship the idol, and face the consequences; or bow down and worship, and abandon their faith. Daniel's three friends, Shadrach, Meshach and Abednego, made the first choice and refused to worship. The consequences were immediate. They were thrown into a fiercely burning furnace – incineration the payment for loyalty to their faith.

Perhaps you know the story? Instead of being consumed by the flames, they stroll calmly through them. To his astonishment, King Nebuchadnezzar spots not three men walking in the fire, but four, and in a memorable statement gasps that 'the fourth looks like a son of the gods' (v. 25). Shadrach, Meshach and Abednego are released and granted permission to worship their God, for, as Nebuchadnezzar says, 'no other god can save in this way' (v. 29). It is rousing stuff.

The conversation this trio had with Nebuchadnezzar before being thrown into the furnace is significant and tells us much about them. In verse 16 they argue that they do not need to justify their refusal to worship the idol to Nebuchadnezzar. The subtext is clear: Nebuchadnezzar is not God, and therefore any command from him is of lesser importance than a command from Yahweh. In verse 17 they affirm their belief that God can rescue them from the fiery ordeal that awaits them. More astonishingly, in verse 18 they inform Nebuchadnezzar that even if they are not rescued, they will never bow down to the god Nebuchadnezzar has crafted. In other words, their continued allegiance to God is not dependent on a favourable response to their plight. Even if abandoned, they will continue to worship only Yahweh. There are traces of Job 13:15 here: 'Though he slay me, yet will I hope in him'.

While undoubtedly courageous, their response was not subtle, and it infuriated Nebuchadnezzar. As verse 19 puts it, 'his attitude towards them changed'.

This is principled leadership.

Principled leaders know what they stand for. They know where to draw the line and will not cross it – even if it costs them their life. While our lives are less likely to be at stake, our job might be, and promotional opportunities often are. We need to know our principles in advance. I have often said to budding leaders: 'Know what you would resign over. Don't decide that lightly but do decide it firmly, for if you don't, you are likely to settle for unacceptable compromises that will haunt you in the longer term.'

It has always taken both courage and deep conviction to be a principled leader. In an age when so many things are considered relative, it is easy to imagine that if our convictions prove too costly, we will be able to find alternative ones. This passage will have none of this.

Given the seriousness of firm convictions, it is important that we settle on the right ones. Sometimes we confuse our preferences with principles and fight hard to have things our way, when a closer analysis shows that we are simply fighting for what we prefer and that no deep principles are at stake. It is also easy to confuse convictions with cultural bias. We have often been shaped by our subculture, and struggle to acknowledge that other ways of doing things could be valid. Again, this will set us up for disappointment.

Leaders need a clear vision to guide and direct them. Without one, their journey is likely to be confused. But they also need carefully considered convictions; otherwise, when they reach their goal, they find it empty because of the many compromises made along the way.

The account of Shadrach, Meshach and Abednego is a reminder that Daniel's trusted aides were also outstanding leaders. There is something about a strong leader that brings out the best in others. On their own, perhaps none of this trio would have found the courage to challenge Nebuchadnezzar. But by working together they discovered they had the strength to live in the light of their convictions – and they did so regardless of the personal cost. The book of Daniel is not simply a story of a fine leader. It is the story of a group of fine leaders who inspire one another.

This story has a happy ending. Verse 30 tells us that the three friends are promoted. The reward of good leadership is to be able to lead at a higher level. But we should not forget the proviso that Shadrach, Meshach and Abednego had inserted. Even if this had not turned out well (and who would have thought it would when they were thrown into the furnace?), they would not have abandoned their hope in Yahweh. Such unconditional loyalty is rare and is something we should ponder in an age of fickle commitments.

**In the lions' den**

We come now to what is probably the most famous story of Daniel – his safe encounter with lions. Let's recount what happens.

A new king, Darius, is now in power, Nebuchadnezzar having died, and his son Belshazzar having been overthrown and killed as the Medes and the Persians became the new superpower and Babylon slipped off the scene. Daniel was an influential leader under three kings, and it says much about him that he managed to speak into each of these different contexts. He did so by consistently remaining true both to his calling and to who he was. Though we may not realize it, sometimes the greatest blessing we can be to others is by being a consistently godly person in every season of life. Some people feel that they should change who they are in the light of changing circumstances, but it often works the other way round, with changing circumstances helping to establish whether we are people with genuine convictions and enduring qualities, or whether our character and principles are as changeable as the weather.

In this story, Daniel comes across what is sometimes called the 'tall poppy syndrome'.[1] Daniel 6:1–2 informs us that Daniel was initially one of three 'chief ministers' in charge of 120 'satraps' (provincial governors) serving under the victorious new king, Darius. However, his God-given ability and commitment to his work quickly sees him soar above the others, and in no time the king plans to put him in charge of all his affairs. Jealous of his advancement, but unable to match his performance, the other satraps and administrators plot against Daniel. Finding him closed to bribes and corruption, they decide to use his faith against him. This was a realm in which Daniel would never compromise, and they knew it. They tricked King Darius into signing a decree that made it illegal to pray to anyone other than the king for a thirty-day period. Even if the legislation had only been valid for a day, Daniel would not have complied, though they probably made it thirty days to be sure of catching him in this novel act of civil disobedience – praying to God.

As so often happens, the satraps were using the king's vanity to trap him, for Darius was fond of Daniel and had come to depend on him. The thought of having everyone pray to him blinded Darius to the obvious risks. An old idiom says, 'They flatter only to deceive', and it applies here. Romans 12:3 advises us to think of ourselves with sober judgement, and we should be cautious when excessive praise comes our way. I am not implying that we should never enjoy a compliment, but leaders are best served when they are well grounded in the reality of both their strengths and their weaknesses. If we don't know our strengths, we may not use them, and if we are not alert to our weaknesses, they will undo us.

Darius's vanity sees him fall for this ploy, and all too predictably he inadvertently signs a death warrant for his friend, for Daniel's response was entirely consistent with his long-established pattern. Hearing the decree that prayer is illegal for thirty days, he continues to pray from an open window facing Jerusalem. He does this not once, but three times each day (Dan. 6:10). Naturally the satraps rush to King Darius to report Daniel, first ensuring that he affirms that his decree is irrevocable (Dan. 6:12). Rather unwisely, the laws of the Medes and Persians could not be revoked – and we should guard against getting ourselves into situations that trap rather than release us. Distressed though he is at having to have Daniel thrown into the lions' den, Darius believes no other option is open to him. One of the hardest moments of leadership is when you see your decisions backfire and spark consequences you never intended. This is one of those devastating moments for Darius. Even kings can find themselves trapped.

Believing no other option is open, Darius assigns Daniel to death. Daniel 6:16 records the rather bizarre wish (or was it a prayer?) offered by Darius on Daniel's behalf: 'May your God, whom you serve continually, rescue you!' In other words, Darius is praying for Daniel – and Daniel is being thrown to the lions for having prayed. As is often said, it's a funny old world, and if you search for consistency you probably won't find it.

The rest of the story is well known. The lions ignored Daniel and he spent an uneventful night with them. The king could not sleep, and in the morning when he discovered Daniel was alive, he had him released, ordering that Daniel's place in the den now be taken by those who had plotted against him. The appetite of the lions immediately returned, and it is best not to dwell on the fate of those who found themselves in their den, for it was assuredly not happy.

What does this famous account tell us about spiritual leadership? Imagine yourself in Daniel's position. Daniel 6:10 tells us that on hearing of the decree forbidding prayer, Daniel 'went home to his upstairs room where the windows opened towards Jerusalem. Three times a day he got down on his knees and prayed, giving thanks to his God, just as he had done before.' Verse 11 adds an additional detail. When those plotting against him went to trap him, they 'found Daniel praying and asking God for help'.

Note what Daniel doesn't do. He doesn't contemplate obeying this new decree. Abandoning God was never an option for him. He had adopted a rhythm of life which involved public prayer three times a day. He stuck to the pattern that had served him through the decades. Some principles are not up for negotiation, and Daniel knows which ones they are. This does not mean he was an inflexible, rigid personality, for such qualities do not serve leaders well. But Daniel was able to discriminate between what was of primary and secondary importance. Prayer had never been of secondary importance in his life, and there was no risk of this changing now.

Also notice the content of his prayer. Verse 10 informs us that he started by giving thanks to God. It would have been understandable if Daniel had first rushed to intercession: 'Lord, please help me. This is a desperate situation!' Instead, Daniel opts to remember the larger context of his life and the causes he has for gratitude. Perhaps he reminded himself that even if his death was imminent, he still had much to be grateful for. His life had already been remarkable, and if the circumstances were now about to change, it did not mean that he should forget to be thankful. Gratitude is a spiritual virtue, grounded in our trust in God's goodness and love. Whatever a particular day brings (and even if it brings our death), the broader context of our life should be gratitude to God, or to quote Job 13:15 again, 'Though he slay me, yet will I hope in him'. In 1 Thessalonians 5:18, the apostle Paul instructs us to 'give thanks in all circumstances'. Perhaps Paul had Daniel in mind when he wrote this.

Not that Daniel does not ask God for help, as verse 11 makes clear. Having thanked God, Daniel turns to his own plight. We don't know exactly what Daniel asked for. Did he ask that God would give him the strength to remain faithful in an impossible situation? Did he ask that God would rescue him? Did he ask God to change the minds of his enemies? Perhaps he did all three, and possibly more.

We have no record of what Daniel said to his captors. The first words we hear from him are at the other side of the ordeal. They are significant. After a sleepless night imagining the slaughter of his friend, King Darius rushes to the lions' den and anxiously calls out to see if Daniel is alive: 'Has your God, whom you serve continually, been able to rescue you from the lions?' (v. 20). Daniel replies: 'May the king live for ever!' (There is nothing wrong with a little diplomacy!) 'My God sent his angel, and he shut the mouths of the lions. They have not hurt me, because I was found innocent in his sight' (vv. 21–22).

This goes to the heart of the matter. Daniel's first concern was that he was found innocent in God's sight. That was his first allegiance. It was the theme of his life. God first, and then everything else will find its proper place.

In an age when many leaders rely on quick fixes and leadership gimmicks, Daniel points us back to basics. Theologians sometimes speak of living *coram Deo* – a Latin expression reminding us that we live 'before the face of God'. Leaders are often acutely aware that they live before the face of others and are desperate to impress followers. Ultimately, however, we live before an audience of One.[2] It is God's verdict on our life that counts, and it is God's affirmation we should seek. Leaders who get this right lead from clear principles and are guided by priorities that matter. They lead a little like Daniel.

**For reflection**

1. What do you admire most about Daniel? Why?
2. How do you differentiate between holding to an important principle and being stubborn and inflexible?
3. What are you willing to resign over? Why?

# 9

# Mary: A Leader from the Second Chair

His mother said to the servants, 'Do whatever he tells you.'

*John 2:5*

Not everyone has the title 'leader', but with some people you look back and realize how great their influence has been, and that things would have been fundamentally different without them. I think Mary is one of those people – someone who led from the second chair, someone who had enormous influence even though she never held the number-one position.

Mary is a figure of much controversy within Christianity, the debate usually centring on the level of honour and veneration she should be shown. For Protestants this is a matter of some sensitivity, and they may quickly accuse Roman Catholic and Orthodox Christians of attaching too much importance to her and suggest that they have fallen into the trap of worshipping Mary instead of Jesus. They note that Mary, despite her important role, was always human, and to worship any human being, however noble, is a form of blasphemy (yes, feelings about this do run high). Those accused are bewildered by the scant attention Protestants pay to Mary, especially as Luke 1 affirms her as one who is 'highly favoured' (v. 28), notes that the 'Lord is with [her]' (v. 28) and that she is 'blessed . . . among women' (v. 42), and reports her own words concerning herself: 'all generations will call me blessed' (v. 48). Not too surprising when you remember that out of all other women, Mary was the one chosen to be *Theotokos*, the God-Bearer or Mother of God. You can't (or shouldn't) gloss over that too quickly. Nor should you forget that

Mary's 'yes' to the archangel Gabriel is forever the model for our response to God: '"I am the Lord's servant," Mary answered. "May your word to me be fulfilled"' (v. 38). You can't top that. Mary was probably a teenager at this time, yet her spiritual formation and maturity was deep and profound.

Though rightly in the shadow of her son, Mary's own story is remarkable. Engaged to be married to a man who was probably many years older, Mary has a life-changing encounter with an angel. She will be the mother of God, the one who will feel him slowly growing in her womb, who has to ensure that he is fed, burped, changed, nurtured and guided in the right paths. Have you ever wondered what it would be like to teach Bible stories to God?

She gives birth far away from her family – cattle and sheep her main support during the birth process. There is little money, and at Jesus' dedication the couple select the offering allowed only to those too poor to do more: 'a pair of doves or two young pigeons' (Luke 2:24; Lev. 12:6–8). Perhaps she told this story to Jesus, and as he sensed the deep embarrassment it had caused her, it might have spurred him to later announce that the widow's mite was as valuable to God as the gold of the wealthy (Mark 12:41–44). A period as a refugee in Egypt follows. Don't say that too quickly. You won't if you have been a refugee or if you have ever had a meaningful conversation with someone who has been. It is harrowing to have to flee for your life, not knowing where you are going or where you will find shelter. To do so with a baby, well . . . let your imagination fill in the details.

Not that the Bible paints an endlessly glossy portrait of Mary. With wry humour it informs us that after taking the 12-year-old Jesus to Jerusalem to celebrate the Passover, Mary and Joseph accidentally leave him behind, Luke 2:44 telling us that they had simply assumed he was somewhere in the returning crowd. They travel a full day without noticing his absence. In the end it takes them three days to find him. Seriously! And you thought you had some bad parenting moments.

It is likely that shortly after this, Mary's husband Joseph dies. Her oldest son, Jesus, carries on her husband's craft of carpentry. Perhaps at this point Mary assumes she faces an ordinary life. Widows were common in Israel, and most often the eldest son looked after them. She probably battled to make sense of the promises made about Jesus as she watched him design a dining-room table or repair a local farmer's plough. She might have heaved a sigh of relief at this, for there is much to be said for a quiet life, though probably she sensed it was simply a brief respite and wondered when it would all change.

Two suggestive asides in the gospels give us a deeper insight into Mary.

The first takes place at a wedding in Cana. Perhaps you remember the story, found in John 2:1–11?

Weddings in the ancient world were even more impressive than they are today. The celebrations straddled several days; sometimes they lasted a week. The cost was considerable, and as hospitality was highly prized, the guest list was usually large. This was a wedding to which Jesus and his disciples had been invited. Think about that. According to John 1, Jesus has only just called his team of disciples together, so it is perfectly possible that the original invitation had been to 'Jesus plus one', but Jesus' plus one turns out to be plus twelve. This would not have been unusual for that time, but it did make catering very tricky! Whatever the reason, insufficient wine had been provided for the size of the group, and the bridal couple and their family face the embarrassment of having inadequately provided for their guests.

It is interesting that Mary quickly spots the dilemma. Perhaps she was that kind of person – someone who notices all that is going on around her and is immediately alert to awkward situations that require kindly intervention. Her response is to inform Jesus of the problem, verse 3 recording her statement, 'They have no more wine.' Jesus' response in verse 4 makes it clear that he did not view this as an idle piece of gossip but as a plea for action, and he pushes back in the way sons often do when they sense their mothers are involving them in someone else's problem: 'Why do you involve me?' He follows this with an intriguing comment: 'My hour has not yet come.'

What is going on here and what does it tell us about Mary, and her leadership style?

For a start it affirms that Mary has confidence in Jesus' ability to make a difference. This is the first of the recorded miracles of Jesus – but perhaps she had seen others which we have no record of, or it could be that he so routinely sorted things out that she was confident he would do so in this situation. Though it is uncertain, there is some speculation that this might have been a marriage of a family relative, so the stakes could have been high, making Mary keen to find a way out of the faux pas. Regardless, what is clear is that she believes the involvement of Jesus will make a difference and she is keen to get him involved. There might have been a strong element of motherly pride, Mary inwardly thinking, 'Now everyone will see what my boy can do.' Quietly, but firmly, she is pushing Jesus into the limelight.

Jesus' challenge back is significant: 'My hour has not yet come.' In essence Jesus is noting that once he starts performing miracles in public there will be no going back. He will attract attention, and being the centre of attention when you belong to a nation conquered by the Romans would have no happy outcome. Mary is unlikely to have realized what she was catapulting Jesus towards – fame, but also the price of fame, which in those troubled times was sometimes crucifixion. This was an age when it was safer to be invisible.

What is especially interesting is that despite his protest, Jesus does what Mary asks. She has pushed him into public attention, but after his initial hesitation, he dives right in. There is no return from this path.

From a leadership perspective we can argue that Mary was leading from the second chair. She knew what needed to be done, and she used her influence to make it happen. Many leaders have no formal role or position but are conscious of the influence they have and who they have it with. In one way or another they use it to get the required outcome. Mary wanted an embarrassment-free wedding. She was unable to achieve this herself but was willing to use her one strategic contact (if we can speak of Jesus as a strategic contact!) to ensure the desired result. Her motivation is other focused. She doesn't get anything from this, other than a mild rebuke from Jesus at this minor act of pushiness, but it is a price she is willing to pay to protect the reputation of her friends. This is an act of genuine kindness, and it is thoughtfully executed. We can learn a lot from it.

What are we to make of Jesus' pushback, 'My hour has not yet come'? Does it mean that Mary was out of line, insensitively pushing her son in a direction that ultimately cost him everything?

This is an unlikely explanation. After all, Jesus had very recently called his disciples together. It was clear that a new chapter was beginning. Perhaps Mary does the most remarkable thing that any parent can do: she opens the door to this new chapter for him. While it certainly cost Jesus his life, it was not without cost for Mary. When she and Joseph had dedicated Jesus at the temple, Simeon had warned her of the day when 'a sword will pierce your own soul too' (Luke 2:35). By pushing Jesus forward, she sets the clock racing towards that day.

In her own way Mary is also providing some reassurance to Jesus. Even though he had called his disciples together, perhaps he wondered if it really was the right time. Mary's invitation is an affirmation that it is indeed time, and that his status as an obscure carpenter from Nazareth is about to end. Mary might not have been the key player, but her engagement would have been a reassuring sign to Jesus that now was the time to begin his mission in earnest.

You could argue that this makes the next encounter with Mary and Jesus' brothers a little confusing. We find it in Mark 3:21 and 31. Jesus' ministry was galloping ahead, and large crowds gathered to hear him and to witness his miracles. Probably anxious that he would both exhaust himself and run foul of the ruling authorities, Jesus' family try to get him to leave Capernaum and come home with them to Nazareth. We might imagine that they dramatically tell the crowd, 'He is out of his mind' (Mark 3:21).

What are we to make of this account? It is a little devastating to have your family speak against you, and in case you think that Mary was not part of this scene, Mark 3:31–32 makes it clear that she was there as well. Having pushed him into commencing his public ministry, she is now trying to shut it down.

Probably this was an act of genuine concern on Mary's part. She had the eyes of a loving mother and could see what the crowd did not. The relentless demands of the masses and the frequent opposition from the religious leaders took their toll on Jesus. Mark 3:20 tells us that the large crowds had made it impossible for either Jesus or his disciples to eat. The gospel writers tell us that there were many times when Jesus attempted to slip away from the crowds to be alone. Most often his efforts were thwarted. Mary wants to protect him. While Jesus was fully divine, he was also fully human, and the fully human Jesus was thoroughly exhausted. His family were extremely worried on his behalf. Leading from the second chair, Mary tries to create a safe space for Jesus. This might have been misguided, but her motivation was not.

Another important factor would have been the growing fame of Jesus. While many of us long for fame and fortune, there are times in history when fame is a curse, leaving us exposed and vulnerable. We are spotted far too easily, and those who are noticed can become scapegoats for the failed agenda of others. This is especially so when they challenge the status quo, as Jesus did on a daily (sometimes hourly) basis. Jesus is travelling a dangerous path, and Mary wants him to stop before he has travelled too far along that route.

It is all in vain. Jesus' mission was always intended to include the cross. It was not the unforeseen outcome of his ministry but lay at the heart of why he came. While Jesus fully understood this, Mary did not. It is a sobering truth that became increasingly clear to her.

Notice the goodness of Mary's intention in this. She does her best to help and protect. Others were unconcerned that Jesus was worn out, and didn't give a second thought about the danger they placed him in. Mary is that most valuable of leaders from the second chair. They see the key leader as a person, not a symbol. They act to lighten their load and they look out for them and their needs.

Mary's concerns were well founded, for as we know, Jesus' ministry leads to his crucifixion. It is here that we see perhaps the most poignant portrait of Mary, summarized in eight haunting words in John 19:25: 'Near the cross of Jesus stood his mother . . .' There is a world of sadness here. But notice the detail. Mary does not watch at a safe distance. She does not 'do a Peter' and deny ever having known Jesus. She not only comes to the crucifixion, but also stands in solidarity with Jesus at the cross – right next to the cross. She was with him at his birth, and she is with him at his death.

These then are five portraits we have of Mary: Mary without adequate shelter in Bethlehem, and soon to be a refugee in Egypt; Mary the forgetful mother, assuming Jesus was somewhere around; Mary the pushy mother, wanting her son's special skills to be noticed and his miracle-performing ministry to begin; Mary the anxious mother, wanting to protect her son from the risks of his mission; Mary the heartbroken mother, standing close to the cross of Jesus.

What do these five portraits teach us about the spiritual dynamics of leadership?

You might question if Mary is actually a leader, but clearly she is. Her impact on the church is enormous, with more churches named after her than any of the disciples.

First, Mary reminds us that leading and following are closely interwoven. A distinctive of Christian leaders is that they are followers first and need to be responsive to the guidance of Scripture and the leadership of the Spirit. This is a profound truth, and a strong Christian distinctive. Christian leaders have the confidence to lead only because they are led.

Second, Mary demonstrates 'servant leadership' or leadership on behalf of others. She is constantly looking out for others, be that an embarrassed wedding host or an exhausted son. She is not looking for what she can get for herself, and indeed, as Simeon noted shortly after Jesus' birth, the most significant impact of Jesus' ministry for Mary was that a sword pierced her own heart.

There are other ways in which we can look at the spiritual leadership exercised by Mary. People sometimes compliment the parents of a successful child by saying, 'The apple doesn't fall far from the tree.' Parents do impact their children. While Jesus often talks about his relationship with his father (and he was thinking of God, not Joseph), it does not take much sensitivity to notice the impact of his mother, Mary.

Remember, Jesus grew up in a world that had only known patriarchy. Women's voices were not encouraged, and their insights were overlooked. Despite this, Jesus was unusually sensitive to the everyday struggles of the women of his time.

There is the dramatic account of the woman caught in adultery. Seeing the male crowd gawking at this shamed woman, Jesus deflects attention from her (probably) naked body by drawing in the sand. He announces that anyone without sin can commence stoning the woman to death, which was the accepted penalty for adultery at the time. By forcing the men to examine their own hearts, he moves them from outrage to introspection. Rather than judging others, and this woman in particular, he suggests that they judge their own self. I wonder if he had heard his mother lament the hypocrisy of men, who in this example had been quick to judge the woman while letting her male partner slip away without penalty. It's part of the routine hypocrisy of a patriarchal society, but Jesus doesn't let it pass. I suspect we have Mary to thank for this.

Or what about Jesus choosing a Samaritan to be the hero in the story of the Good Samaritan? Where did Jesus learn this openness to the outsider? Was it perhaps the case that Mary told Jesus about the hospitality the family had been shown when they were refugees in Egypt? Had she quietly shaped his attitudes to be open and inclusive?

Or in the interchange between the two sisters Mary and Martha (Luke 10:38–42), why is Jesus so quick to affirm Mary's decision to sit and listen to the teaching of Jesus? In an era when it was considered a waste of time to teach women, Jesus takes a different line. Unusually for the time, Jesus never stereotypes or belittles women. He selects women to be the first witnesses to his resurrection. Is it too much to imagine the influence of Mary in this? Probably not.

While we are quick to affirm the divinity of Jesus, the Bible reminds us of his humanity. Strange though it may sound, Luke 2:52 reminds us that as Jesus grew up, he 'grew in wisdom and stature, and in favour with God and man'. How can God grow in wisdom? It's an intriguing question, but I have little doubt that Mary would quickly interject and remind us of the many things she taught Jesus.

Not all leadership takes place in the limelight. The mentor of a promising young worker might see them fly far higher than the mentor ever did, but their role in the success of their protégé should not be overlooked. In a world where women were forced to take a background role, Mary reminds us that leading from the second chair is a valid form of leadership.

Stephen Covey notes that a characteristic of highly effective people is that they begin with the end in view.[1] He suggests that we ask what we would like people to say at our funeral, and then live in accordance with the affirmations that will one day be made. By this standard, Mary's life is truly exceptional. She is usually remembered as the greatest of the saints, and is recognized not just in Christianity but in Islam as well, and is often mentioned in the Qur'an. Her wholehearted 'yes' to the call of God on her life has shaped the course of history. Though her role was largely in the background, she is a spiritual giant we can all learn from.

**For reflection**

1. What stands out for you from the life of Mary? In what way is she a role model for you? What do you admire most about her?
2. Have you ever led from the second chair? If so, what skills did it require from you? What impact did it have?
3. In what ways is Mary's leadership a model for all leaders?

# Section C

# Leadership Practices to Follow

# 10

## What Is Leadership? A Seven 'S' Inventory

Here is a trustworthy saying: whoever aspires to be an
overseer desires a noble task.

*1 Tim. 3:1*

We have spoken about the importance of spiritual formation for
leadership and looked at three outstanding leaders from the Bible.
But what exactly is leadership? This is both a reasonable and an important question.

Kevin Kruse defines leadership as 'a process of social influence,
which maximizes the efforts of others, towards the achievement of
a goal'.[1] It's a helpful definition. Note the three parts. Leadership is
about social influence; it is about maximizing effort; and it is about
achieving goals – though I would suggest that something more than
goals is achieved (for goals can be small and sporadic); rather, the
achievement is in moving a group so that their efforts all work towards attaining the mission and vision of the group. Leadership is
about things that happen, and happen as a result of influence that
is well used, motivating others so they offer their best and providing
clear direction.

Although there is no 'one size fits all' rule for leadership (and
be very suspicious of anyone who suggests that there is), there are
some things that most leaders do. For a few individuals, leadership
comes instinctively, and they are able to quickly read the situation
they find themselves in and intuitively plot the way ahead. But for
most people it takes great effort and careful thought as they put
aside their natural fears and inhibitions and assess what their group

needs to do to move forward. For all it is about a journey – going somewhere – leading.

By its very name, leadership implies stepping out in front. It might be the literal leading of a group of travellers on a tour, pointing the path ahead and looking out for anxious followers who are carefully keeping up in case they get left behind. More often it is figurative, as we think of what lies ahead and wonder how to mobilize people and resources to ensure we make a positive impact. Leaders recognize that the future is theirs to shape, and rather than passively accepting their fate or that of their group as inevitable, they step into the work of building the world they want to see. They calculate what it will take and realistically evaluate both the assets and deficits they face in their present context, but their eye is fixed on the journey ahead and on the vision they need to cast to ensure others will accompany them along the way.

Leaders play many different roles, but the best juggle at least seven. For ease of memory when discussing these roles, I will resort to alliteration. That's often not a good idea, as it can mean you force important concepts into unfortunate labels, but in this instance I think it works. Here are my seven 'S' words for leaders. A leader should be a Stirrer, Saint, Servant, Shepherd, Steward, See-er and Sage.

I'll unpack each of these shortly, but in case your initial response is, 'That is simply not me – count me out', can I urge you to persevere? Many think of leadership as something mystical and beyond their reach. When we name what leaders do, we make it less mysterious and it becomes more attainable. As we explore the seven roles leaders play, instead of saying 'That is so unlike me', why not be curious and ask, 'Why not me? Is there really anything that stops me from aiming at this?'

Why am I prompting you to discover the leader inside you?

Because leaders make a difference. They really matter. And most of us can make more of a difference than we think. Rather than being afraid of the challenges we might face, we should be afraid of what might happen if we don't take them on.

The church is facing a leadership vacuum. Many of our leaders have led from muddled motives and we are paying the price. While we should lament what has gone wrong, we must also learn from it. The leaders we need are those who will work at being both stirrers and saints. Yes, *work* at it – for we cannot passively assume that everything will simply fall into our lap. But neither of the two roles is negotiable. Stirrers who are not saintly will deeply damage God's work in the world. Those who are simply saintly will bless a small circle of people, but the circle may be too small to have the impact it should.

About 2,700 years ago God asked a trembling Isaiah, 'Whom shall I send? And who will go for us?' (Isa. 6:8). To his astonishment, Isaiah heard himself answering, 'Here am I. Send me!' The need today is every bit as great as it was then. Could it be that God is asking you the same probing question? If not you, who?

Let's dig into the seven key roles the best leaders play.

**The leader as stirrer**

Stirrer: One who is willing to dive in and be a change agent

Leaders are stirrers. By that I mean they don't passively accept the way things are. They stir things up. They get people moving and asking questions they hadn't previously considered. Sometimes they align people and resources in fresh ways so that new options become possible. They paint a picture of what the future could look like, and they motivate people to go on the journey with them.

This is the part of leadership many find daunting. But we should ask 'Why?'

When thinking of the leader as a stirrer, many people think of a dynamic, charismatic leader, someone who is a little larger than life, who is naturally confident, articulate and bounding in energy. They feel that they themselves do not measure up. And few people do match the stereotypes that are often tritely paraded around as having what it takes to be a leader.

In reality there are many ways to be a successful stirrer. If you are the naturally charismatic leader of the caricatures, wonderful. Use your giftedness to lead well, and pay special attention to the following notes on the leader as saint, servant, shepherd and sage, for there is something about being a naturally charismatic leader that opens the temptation to sidestep these important roles. If these dimensions of leadership are ignored, the outcome is invariably negative.

While leadership comes naturally and easily to a few, most must work at it. Even those who seem to find it effortless have usually applied themselves more than might be obvious. Long-term successful leadership requires discipline and tenacity. You need the resilience to bounce back from disappointment, and the humility to own up to mistakes and learn from them.

Part of the discipline of leadership is a careful evaluation of the current situation, and prayerful reflection on the church's or group's position. As a stirrer, the leader needs to engage in what Otto Scharmer calls 'generative listening', which is listening with the intention of hearing the highest possible future for a group or organization.[2] It is as though when we think about the future we hear it calling to us, alerting us to its possibilities.

Generative listening requires us to play things forward two, five, ten or even more years, and to imagine what we could and should look like then if . . .

If what?

The leader as stirrer anticipates what it will take to get to that desired future. If we want to be at this point in five years' time, what must we start doing now to get there? Generative listening works backwards from the desired future. It is a discipline, not an instinct. It is something we must do, rather than something mystical. It takes hard work as we look at social trends, demographics, our current resources and the environment in which we are located. It requires much discussion and some social imagination. If we do not have the necessary skills, we can invite those who do to join us.

Being a stirrer starts with a gentle impatience with the present. It is not necessarily that everything is *wrong*, but that it is less than it could be. Those who are fully satisfied with what is already in place are unlikely to lead, because when leaders lead, change is never far away. And you don't push for change if you already have all you want.

Perhaps you again say, 'But I am not naturally a stirrer. I am a fairly accepting person and like to simply fit in.'

That might well be true, but in your quieter moments do you catch yourself longing for something better, for something more? Do you sense that if things were to start again you would do them differently? That's the stirrer inside you. It's the voice of appropriate discontent. It is not about being ungrateful or criticizing what others have done. It is about recognizing that life is dynamic and that things that don't change usually slip slowly towards decay. It is also the voice of possibility, reminding you that you are called to be a player in life, not a spectator. Listen to it creatively and it will help to unearth the leader inside you. It might well be the voice of God calling out to you.

A qualification needs to be added here. Some people are instinctive stirrers. They get people worked up, perhaps playing on their discontent and frustrations. They point out the faults in others and the flaws in the present system. They are quick to help people spot what is wrong, but don't acknowledge what is right or the challenges that the present context might create. They are stirrers, but their stirring leads in no constructive direction, for they point to no realistic path ahead. When they leave the group, everyone knows what is wrong but has little idea of what to do about it.

This is not the leadership I am talking about, for that is not being a leader but a troublemaker! Leaders stir things up, but they constructively channel the momentum that is created. It is not stirring for the sake of creating discontent, but to get people to walk along a better path. Leaders stir, but then they point a way ahead. They help people to catch a vision of a brighter future, one which can be reached by following a challenging but manageable pathway.

## The leader as saint

Saint: One who bows the knee to Jesus and genuinely wants to do God's will

You might instinctively dismiss the notion that a leader should be a saint, and be emphatic that if this is a requirement, leadership will never come your way. But let me push back.

According to the Bible, all Christians are supposed to be saints. Paul often addresses his letters to the 'saints' at various locations: Corinth (1 Cor. 1:2), Ephesus (Eph. 1:1), Philippi (Phil. 1:1). He uses a Greek word, *agios*, which essentially means someone who is holy. While you might reply, 'Exactly – saints are the super-holy', remember that the word 'holy' has a simple meaning. It is someone or something that is set aside for God.

Things can be holy. The utensils in the Jewish temple were considered holy because they were set apart for the worship of God. Though the dishes were capable of being used at any other meal, or the basins could have been utilized for washing hands in many other contexts, they had been specially assigned to be used in the temple as part of the worship of God. They were therefore 'holy' because they were for the exclusive use of the temple. While they could have been put to use in other settings, they weren't. That is why they were considered desecrated when conquering hordes destroyed the temple and used them for other purposes.

The leader as saint is someone who has responded to the call of God on their life and is genuinely trying to live for God and do what they believe God wants them to. They will not do it perfectly, and will often make mistakes, but their basic intent is genuine. A saint is someone who sincerely attempts to put God first in their life, who is willing to pray, 'God, here is my life. Please use it as you see fit.' They see being in relationship with and available to God as the primary purpose of their life.

Living as a saint is an ongoing invitation. In Romans 12:1 Paul urges us to offer our bodies as a 'living sacrifice' to God. His idea that the sacrifice is a living one is challenging. There is no one supreme act of self-renunciation that leaves us forever able to claim the title 'saint'. Rather it is in the flow and decision-making of our everyday life that our sainthood is established. Each time we allow our allegiance to Jesus to shape our words or actions, we are walking the path of holiness. When our default is to say 'yes' to what our allegiance to Jesus requires, we are making genuine progress.

The leader as saint knows that they are led. While they might report to a church board or to denominational officials, they ultimately report to a higher power. They are not independent operators and are deeply conscious of their need to be accountable. They know that they must lead a life worthy of their calling (Eph. 4:1) and that they will answer to the One who called them. That does not make them distrustful of the board they report to, but it helps them to put their decision-making in a wider context.

While this might sound noble and perhaps even idealistic, it is simply what every Christian is called to. If you are saying that you cannot be a leader because you are not a saint (in the biblical sense of the word), then your first challenge is a spiritual one, not a leadership one. Commit yourself more deeply to Jesus. Take your spiritual growth seriously. And remember that everything is spiritual. In Colossians 3:17 Paul instructs us that whatever we do, be it in our words or deeds, we must do it all in the name of Jesus. Six verses on, Paul extends this idea further as he tells us that our actions must be done with all our heart, as though we are working for Jesus (Col. 3:23).

Most Christian leaders start out acutely aware of their need for God's help on the journey ahead and deeply committed to being a spiritual leader. Often the sheer pace of leadership sees this commitment slip. It is not as though a leader wakes up one day and says, 'From now on I will be less holy'; it is more that in the whirl of life, priorities shift without our noticing. The change becomes apparent over a longer period. It is dangerous when a leader's popularity and platform has grown more quickly than their character or relationship with God. The best leaders take their call to be a saint with the utmost seriousness, and prioritize it, being willing to undergo regular spiritual audits to ensure that they remain *agios*, holy, a saint, one set aside for God.

## The leader as servant

> Servant: One who puts the needs of others ahead of their own and tries to help meet them

All Christians are called to serve or to be servants. We are called to serve God, to serve one another and to serve the world God loves so deeply. Being someone who serves makes one an obedient Christian servant. Being someone who serves through their leadership makes one a servant leader. I am not trying to quibble over words here or to be clever, but to make an important distinction. All Christians are called to serve. Christian leaders are called to serve through their leadership.

To serve a group through the leadership you offer is a difficult and sometimes costly gift. Servant leadership is not about being the first to offer to wash the dishes or carry the rubbish out. Those are acts of valuable service, but they are not inherently leadership actions.

Perhaps this example will help make my point. After a well-attended church event, there are lots of small tasks to be undertaken. Chairs must be packed away, the carpet vacuumed, dishes washed, volunteers thanked and so on. While a servant leader might sometimes raise their hand to help with some of these tasks (which can be fun if they are not what you always do), they know that their deeper responsibility as a leader is to initiate an evaluation of the event. What went well? What didn't? What can be done better next time? Should there be a next time? Does this fit in with our overall direction? What was the mood like? Does anyone need to be followed up on? Has this event opened other doors for us? If so, how should we capitalize on this?

These questions quickly move us to another zone. It isn't about making sure that everything is neatly tidied up, but that the group's vision and mission is furthered through each event. It means we look at everything with the eyes of a leader. This is stretching, as the leader is never fully off duty. If you serve through washing the dishes, when the last dish is put away your task is done and you can put your feet up. But when is the work of a servant leader over?

This is why leaders often wake up in the middle of the night thinking of things that could have been done. It is why most leaders work at putting some boundaries in place so that they can have moments of leisure. But even when 'off duty', servant leaders know that if a genuine and significant need suddenly arose, they would be back at the helm – for it isn't about them, but the group they are committed to serving.

The ultimate servant leader is Jesus. Philippians 2:5–11 describes his downward journey into servant leadership. It reminds us that though Jesus was God, he took on a human form and came to serve, going so far as to die for us, and dying not any death, but a horrifying death on a cross. He died for us – the supreme act of love and selfless service. Leadership that is modelled on the example of Jesus points away from the leader to the needs of the people in their group. The leader's role is to help them to become all God has called them to be. It is a noble and lofty call, and it is certainly not for the narcissistic.

While leadership sometimes confers gifts and privileges on the leader (for leaders are often paid more than others and treated with respect), if this is the motivation for leadership it will backfire badly.

The test of a leader is not who the leader becomes, but who the group they lead becomes.

## The leader as shepherd

Shepherd: One who looks out for others and ensures they are nurtured well

Depending on the translation you work with, you will find the word 'shepherd' over forty times in the Bible (forty-three if you use the King James Version). It is often linked to the leader's role. More remarkably, we are told that Jesus is our good shepherd and that he lays his life down for the sheep (John 10:11–18). This is an astonishing image and one that we would not necessarily associate with being a shepherd. After all, some think that the role of the shepherd is to look after the sheep until their day of slaughter, not the shepherd's day of slaughter.

While the cynical might question the use of shepherding imagery, it is better to ask what aspects of being a shepherd the Bible likens to leadership. No analogies are perfect, and we go astray if we wander from the intent behind an image. In 1 Peter 5:2–4 Peter speaks of Jesus as our 'Chief Shepherd', and Christian leaders as 'shepherds of God's flock', reminding us that the church belongs to God, and that those who are its leaders must take care of those entrusted to them, and assume responsibility for what happens.

Good shepherds look after their flock. They ensure that the sheep are well fed, protected, adequately rested and nurtured (Ps. 23). Leaders who are shepherds do not carelessly engage with those following their lead; rather, they think carefully about what they will need in order to be sustained on the long journey ahead.

While the leader of a small group might be able to do this on their own, those who lead larger churches or organizations often delegate the role of shepherd to others. They may watch over the pastoral needs of those who work most closely with them (usually only a small group), while ensuring that systems are in place to support and enhance the experience of all who are part of their organization. This does not mean that they never stretch or challenge their followers. To the contrary, a normal part of being healthy is to test your limits and enhance your capacity. This does not happen if you are spoon fed or treated as incapable of mature decision-making and accountability. A shepherding leader ensures that their flock is growing, and this is often achieved through exciting and stretching assignments.

While committed to growing all who are part of the group, the shepherd leader is conscious that everyone is vulnerable. We have already explored Genesis 2:7 where the first person created is formed from the dust of the earth and the breath of God. The image is rich. As those who have been animated by the breath of God, we have infinite worth and value. As those shaped from the dust of the earth we are frail, mere dust that can easily be blown away. Holding these two images in creative tension is an important part of shepherding leadership. It is as though we are simultaneously told to expect great things from people and also to expect great disappointments from them. Leaders need to think long and hard about how their organization can bring the best out of its people, while protecting them from their shadow self.

Change is a constant we all face. At the 2018 World Economic Forum, Canadian Prime Minister Justin Trudeau memorably said: 'The pace of change has never been this fast, yet it will never be this slow again.' That he said this before the Covid-19 pandemic is particularly poignant. We are seeing the price tag of this in the dramatic increase in the number of people struggling with anxiety and mood disorders. 'Beyond Blue', an Australia-based organization, reported in 2021 that one in seven Australians (or 14.4%) aged between 16 and 85 had experienced an anxiety disorder in the previous year, and that over one quarter (26.3%) will experience an anxiety disorder at some point in their life. Because leaders are change agents, they need to be acutely aware of this. The change we precipitate might be tipping some of those we serve into anxiety and stress. We need to watch out for those who are particularly vulnerable.

There are important questions that leaders need to ask if they are to shepherd people well. They include the following:

- How will we help them overcome the sense of loss that often accompanies change, even when the change is needed?
- How will we support them when things don't go to plan?
- How will we help them to manage success well? (Remember that the temptations that accompany success are often greater than those which follow a disappointment)
- How will we help them to put appropriate boundaries in place, so that they know when to say 'yes' and when to say 'no'?
- How will we know we are not just using them? Will we value them as individuals and not just for what they can do for our group?
- What value can we add to their life?

These are simply taster questions to help you think like a shepherd leader. Ask them not only on behalf of those who are following your lead, but also for yourself and for your family. Although you are a leader, you are also made of the dust of the earth, and are not exempt from stress, anxiety or panic.

When leaders are under stress, it tends to leak though their organization. They lose the ability to provide the calm leadership the group needs in order to fare well. Groups operate as systems, and if one part of the system is unhealthy it affects the other parts. Shepherding your own needs is consequently an important part of leadership. It is not selfish to plan for long-term viability. While we can manage short bursts when our workload is unreasonable and the demands are high, this is not sustainable over time. Many leaders become progressively weary and lose that special spark of energy and flair that first helped attract people to their lead. There is a haunting perceptiveness in W.B. Yeats's poem 'Easter, 1916', where Yeats (as we noted in a previous chapter) observes that 'Too long a sacrifice / Can make a stone of the heart'. What started as a willing sacrifice can morph into cynicism and bitterness if proper practices of self-care are not implemented.

Shepherd leaders need to be shepherded, and finding a suitable mentor is an important part of a leadership plan. Your mentor can help you see perspectives that are more easily noticed by those who are not buried in the action. Beware of being part of an echo chamber, where the only views allowed are those which affirm what you already believe. Dangerous blind spots grow in those spaces, but a good mentor will enable you to see more widely. They will help you to appreciate what you have, while nudging you towards a wider horizon.

## The leader as steward

> Steward: One who ensures that all resources – human, physical and financial – are responsibly and effectively utilized

All leaders work with paradox. The most common is the 'person–organization' paradox. In other words, every person in your organization matters, but so does the organization. Whose needs should dominate when the needs of the organization conflict with the needs of the person? Another common dilemma is the 'not for profit but balance your budget' paradox, where we know that ministry is not about money and we want to make our services available for free, but then face the challenge that we still have bills to pay, and if they aren't, our entire ministry might be shut down.

These colliding truths point to the importance of the leader as a steward. Stewards juggle conflicting needs and priorities while trying to plot the most humane and responsible path ahead.

I said 'humane' intentionally, for as organizations grow they often lose the personal touch and become removed from the private fears and insecurities of their employees or followers. Though they might claim to be person- or employee-centric, most organizations are primarily concerned for their own well-being. At a certain level this is appropriate (what help is an organization if it no longer exists?), but groups can drift towards becoming ruthless and self-serving without noticing the change until it is very difficult to stop.

When leaders wear their steward hat they ask hard questions and often probe into uncomfortable areas. Rather than accept anecdotal evidence, they start to apply more stringent criteria. They might ask, 'Why do we say things are going well? What's the hard evidence to back the claim?' They might question if the key performance indicators really reflect the mission and values of the group. And they will be unimpressed if there are no key performance indicators!

Judging the effectiveness of Christian ministry is notoriously difficult. There is little agreement on what success looks like. When a church tries to assess if it has had a fruitful year, what does it look for? Is it increased attendance, or the number of people who became Christians through a church programme, or a larger financial offering, or a greater number of volunteers helping at activities, or a busy church schedule, or the completion of a building project? While measurable, these criteria are often rejected as superficial, and critics of hard data usually suggest that we should pay more attention to the growth in spiritual maturity of the congregation. I have no intention of entering into the fray, though I would suggest that we opt for a wide array of criteria – some of it hard data (such as attendance and giving), others more subjective but important (spiritual responsiveness). Regardless of what is used to evaluate success, good stewards know they are accountable, and this requires taking stock of what we are doing and assessing its effectiveness.

There is an additional dimension of stewardship we should think about. While leaders sometimes claim success because they have tangible achievements they can point to (such as a completed building project or increased attendance), economists usually want to dig a little deeper, and raise questions about the overall 'return on investment' (ROI). ROI is a reminder that return is relative to the size of the investment or opportunity. If we work with much, much is required of us. Equally, if we have many opportunities we are equipped to respond to, we should expect a greater return than those who work in a difficult context where the best they can do is to turn hard soil so that there might be a harvest at a later season.

Matthew 25:14–30 is a parable that stewards take to heart. Jesus tells a story of a man going on a long journey who entrusts different sums of money to his three servants. To one he gives five bags of gold, to another two, and to the third, just one. The one with the five bags invests the gold and doubles it to ten bags, the one with two increases it to four, but the final servant buries his single bag of gold in the ground. Predictably, when the master returns he is delighted with the productivity of both the first and second servants but is dismayed that the man with only one bag of gold opted to bury it. He gives this single bag to the man who has doubled what he had to ten, so that servant now has eleven bags. He then allows the man who has four to hold on to them, while the man who made no effort to use what he had has his gold taken from him.

It is not hard to see the implication of the story. We are supposed to use what we have been given – be it five bags of gold, two bags or one bag. While we might think it unfair that some start with more than others, the story emphasizes that no one finishes where they started. The original configuration of five–two–one quickly changes to eleven–four–zero. Life is not static. We are called to be productive stewards of what is in our care. Leaders take their followers on a journey that goes somewhere. It is not a walk in the park – it is directed and focused, and has desired outcomes. As Paul says in 1 Corinthians 9:26, 'I do not run . . . aimlessly'. Leaders are stewards who know they will give account. They ask hard questions, knowing that ultimately facts are friends, and that we must interpret them well and pay close attention to what they are saying.

**The leader as see-er**

See-er: One who anticipates the future and helps to shape it

To lead in the right direction, leaders need to anticipate the future. They see a little earlier and further than others. They develop their ability to play things forward – not so far forward that they get out of touch with their followers, but far enough ahead to avoid or abandon projects that will go nowhere.

To be an effective see-er, the leader needs an external and an internal gaze.

Externally they look at emerging trends, focusing on both megatrends (those enormous changes that impact everyone) and changes that are more specific to their line of work. While operating in the present, leaders are aware that the future moves towards us a day at a time. Things don't just stay as they are, and it is wise to plan for the challenges and opportunities that tomorrow will bring. Failure to do so can be catastrophic, and examples abound.

Think for example of the Kodak company which, after years of leading in all things photographic, failed to pivot towards the changes that came with the advent of digital photography. Kodak spent ten years trying to persuade the public that film cameras were better than digital ones, despite the mounting and increasingly obvious evidence to the contrary. In 2013 they filed for bankruptcy. Although they have since made a modest effort to reinvent themselves, they are a long way off their golden era. Ten wasted years of fighting the inevitable has cost them dearly.

By contrast, Kodak's closest rival at the time, Fujifilm, faced the same challenges but responded positively, seeing in the move to digital the possibility for new markets and different products. They had to make dramatic changes, but their fortunes have soared.

Leaders know that the future is not a passive given. We might prefer to ignore disturbing trends, but that does not make them go away. However, we can be part of shaping the future by the actions we take today.

The leader's gaze should also be internal – looking closely at the group's need to change in order to fare well in the future. A key role is seeing what needs to be put in place to help the group to grow. This might be through staffing up, succession planning, investing wisely or implementing training programmes. It requires a decision on what parts of the present will be held on to, and what will progressively change. It is right to resist some changes, while embracing others. Clearly stated values can make these decisions a little easier, but leaders need to hear the call of the future. They should listen to members of a younger generation and intentionally engage in conversation with them.

In my own leadership I have found it helpful to think of myself as overseeing a chapter of the book the group is writing. Remembering that I am a chapter, not the book, helps to keep things in perspective. There will be many chapters, and the possible options for the coming chapters are shaped by what is done in the present one. I ask where the arc of the story leads. I try to project forward. How should the book end? I then ask, 'What must we do now to make this ending possible?'

It is rather liberating to remember that we are part of a larger story, for in the end leadership is about helping a group discover their role in the story of God. This is the narrative we are all called to participate in, but it is much bigger than any one of us. It doesn't all depend on us, but we are called to be meaningful players in it. It is an enormous privilege to play a part in this story.

## The leader as sage

Sage: One who is wise, learns from all of life and shares it with others

It is impossible to overrate the value of wisdom. While it sometimes comes with age, getting older does not automatically make you wise. Many older people simply repeat the errors they have been making for decades, for unless we are willing to evaluate past actions and attitudes, we are unlikely to learn from experience. Even when we take the time to do such an evaluation, we can deceive ourselves, for if we are confined to an echo chamber where we are only exposed to views compatible with our own, we are unlikely to face the rigorous critique that can lead to growth.

While there is no shortcut to wisdom, there are practices we can adopt that will help us to grow and mature. We can read widely, listen deeply, cultivate curiosity and allow our life experiences to teach us. Psalm 1 discusses the practice of meditating carefully on Scripture and allowing it to produce its fruit in season. Not everything has an instant pay-off, but healthy choices that become habits lead to high dividends.

The best leaders are teachers, because without the ability to teach, what we have discovered remains trapped inside us. In 2 Timothy 2:2 Paul tells us that what we have learned we must pass on to others, who in turn will pass it on to others. This is a significant way of expanding our leadership. Naturally it comes with sobering responsibility, for if what we pass on is substandard or unhelpful, we make things more difficult for the next generation of leaders.

Noel Tichy has written: 'The essence of leading is not commanding, but teaching. It is opening people's eyes and minds. It is teaching them new ways to see the world and pointing them to new goals.'[3]

Many leaders are wise but have not spent enough time crystallizing their insights in a way that is transmittable. Sometimes it helps to capture an insight in a memorable maxim or proverb. Alternatively, conveying truth through stories is also very powerful and provides some flexibility for interpretation as contexts change. Wisdom is for sharing and is part of a leadership legacy. Ask people what they will remember about you, what phrases they associate with you and what key convictions they see in you. These are the things that will be remembered long after you have left.

## Moving from a fixed to a growth mindset

You might well have read these seven descriptions with a sense of frustration or even despair. Your instinct might be that very few of them describe you, or worse, that none of them do! 'That's it,' you may be saying to yourself. 'I know I'm not a leader, and I never will be. It's not my fault, but I can't balance my own budget, let alone be a good steward for others, while the thought of having to be a servant really doesn't inspire me, and being a see-er – well, seriously! I can't even predict what will happen today.'

At this point you face a basic choice. Will you face the future with a fixed or a growth mindset? Those with a fixed mindset view life statically.[4] Either you are intelligent or you are not. Either you have an aptitude for sport or you don't. You are musical or you are not. And you are a leader or you are not.

Those with a fixed mindset place their emphasis on natural ability, but while it is true that some begin tasks or activities with a greater natural aptitude for them than others, those with a fixed mindset overlook the difference made by hard work. They might assume that those who are naturally gifted don't need to practise diligently to be successful in their area of talent. This is simply not true. It takes significant work and practice to develop latent abilities. In addition, with hard work and a non-defensive attitude, most people improve.

This brings us to those who have a growth mindset. They don't expect everything to come naturally. They are keen to grow, and know they won't without effort. Whereas those with a fixed mindset often view hard work as a risk, reasoning that if they try hard at something but don't succeed they show everyone that they are not naturally gifted, those with a growth mindset think about it differently. They reason that the real risk is not putting in enough effort, for without effort why would they expect to succeed?

Let me encourage you to adopt a growth mindset towards leadership. Whatever challenges you face, you can improve. In his book on the seven habits of highly successful people Stephen Covey notes that the first habit is being proactive.[5] Those who are passive do not make a difference. Proactivity is a choice. It comes to those who cultivate the habit of asking, 'What needs to be done to improve this?' By contrast the passive accept the status quo, not factoring in the slow decline that comes with time when settings are not questioned or adjusted.

Notice I spoke of cultivating the 'habit' of asking. Don't under-estimate the power of habits and the importance of examining your habits to ensure that they serve you well. We often assume that life is shaped by the big decisions we make. In reality, most of our life is lived on autopilot, so checking our settings is important. If we have got into the habit of going to bed a little later than we should, and consequently have less energy than we should, we will achieve less than we should. This is entirely predictable. The secret of success, or failure, is linked to our daily routine.

Let's then look more closely at the seven key 'S' qualities of lead-ers. Rate yourself on each of them, but do so with a growth mindset. What do you need to do to improve in this area? Is there a habit that holds you back which you can adjust? Be both realistic and ruthless. In other words, when you need to praise yourself for being strong in an area, do so. And when there are areas to face in which you struggle, do so with honesty and clarity, for both honesty and clarity will be faithful friends as you grow in your leadership. Having the humility and courage to be the best leader you can is an important part of your spiritual growth and maturing. Indeed, tackling some of the habits that hold us back can see us take a spiritual leap. Be it challenging passivity or overcoming a cynical attitude, committing to a growth mindset makes an enormous difference.

---

### For reflection

Rate yourself from 1 to 10 on the seven 'S' qualities of spiritual leaders. A score of 1 means that this is not like you at all, 5 in-dicates that you are much the same as most people in this area, while 10 means it describes you very accurately. Take some time to think how you can proactively improve in each area, and then write some steps down. Be tangible and clear. What would make a difference? How will you hold yourself accountable in each area?

| 'S' leadership quality | My self-rating from 1 to 10 | What I can do to improve |
|---|---|---|
| Stirrer: One who is willing to dive in and be a change agent | | |
| Saint: One who bows the knee to Jesus and genuinely wants to do God's will | | |
| Servant: One who puts the needs of others ahead of their own and tries to help meet them | | |
| Shepherd: One who looks out for others and ensures they are nurtured well | | |
| Steward: One who ensures that all resources – human, physical and financial – are responsibly and effectively utilized | | |
| See-er: One who anticipates the future and helps to shape it | | |
| Sage: One who is wise, learns from all of life and shares it with others | | |

# 11

# Leading Quietly

The first thing Andrew did was to find his brother
Simon and tell him, 'We have found the Messiah' (that
is, the Christ). And he brought him to Jesus.

*John 1:41–42*

In 2013 I published a book on quiet leadership.[1] I was drawn to the
concept as I had noticed that many people back away from leadership because they associate it with larger-than-life characters who
stand out from the crowd. Not identifying with that image, they
assume leadership is not for them.

As someone who blends into the surroundings, I have always
sympathized with those who feel like that. Yet I know that I carry
many significant leadership roles and perform them effectively and
have had good results. I'm a change agent and have usually been able
to usher in change without forming enemies or leaving behind a trail
of disarray and resentment. But larger than life I am not!

I know from my own experience that stereotypical views of leadership are not useful and am keen to help those who are hesitant to
step up for leadership to have the confidence to develop their leadership potential. The more I read, research and observe in this area,
the more hopeful I become. It is possible to lead quietly, and indeed
those who do are often the most effective leaders, especially if it is
genuine results and actual change you are looking for. A growing
body of research suggests that while some leaders are charismatic,
there are many effective leaders who more quietly go about the task
of changing their world.[2]

Did you know that charismatic views of leadership have not always been dominant but sprang into prominence with the shift from rural to urban living? As cities grew larger, it became harder to know who would be able to lead well. Cities were made up of strangers, and people had to find ways to stand out from the crowd. Those who were louder or larger got noticed. Those who were noticed were more likely to be invited to lead. While being self-assertive is often viewed negatively in rural settings, in urban settings it is often the quickest way to climb the ladder.

With these sociological changes, leadership theories started to emphasize qualities that helped people get spotted. Charismatic theories of leadership came into their own. Back in the day when most grew up in a rural setting, people were known from childhood, and their family history in the area dated back for generations. The locals knew who did what well, and who could be trusted with responsibility. It wasn't about who made a powerful first impression, but whose impression stood the test of a few decades and had been proved in difficult circumstances. To become a leader in a rapidly growing city required different skills from those needed for leading a long-settled rural community.

It is, however, one thing to become a leader, and another to effectively continue as a leader year in and year out. Charisma may open doors, but only diligent service keeps them open for the long haul. This has become increasingly recognized, and theories of quiet leadership are now accepted.

One of the pioneers of quiet leadership, Joseph Badaracco, has written: 'Over the course of a career spent studying management and leadership, I have observed that the most effective leaders are rarely public heroes. These men and women aren't high-profile champions . . . They move patiently, carefully, and incrementally.'[3] Later he writes: 'I have come to call these people *quiet leaders* because their modesty and restraint are in large measure responsible for their impressive achievements. And since many big problems can only be resolved by a long series of small efforts, quiet leadership, despite its seemingly slow pace, often turns out to be the quickest way to make an organization – and the world – a better place.'[4]

Not only are quiet leaders effective, but they also find it easier to straddle the tension between being a stirrer and a saint. Knowing that everything doesn't depend on them, and that without God's help they are unlikely to achieve much, prayer comes more naturally. A quiet demeanour also makes it easier to listen to others and to God without constantly interrupting. Deep listening is a key to transformative leadership, and it comes more instinctively to quiet leaders.

Badaracco suggests that there are five virtues closely associated with quiet leadership.[5] They are modesty, restraint, tenacity, interdependence and other-centredness. I will explore each in turn, discussing why they are key to long-term success in leadership. Naturally, simply reading about virtues you might not possess is unlikely to be helpful, so I will also investigate how we can grow in each of these areas.

## Modesty

> Modesty: The quality of being unassuming in self-assessment, and willing to give others credit ahead of yourself

Modesty is a key to personal and organizational growth. Those with an inflated self-opinion are rarely open to change, and don't see the need for a system of feedback to alert them to both blind spots and strengths.

Modesty is not about running yourself down or pretending that you have no contribution to make. In Romans 12:3 Paul urges: 'Do not think of yourself more highly than you ought, but rather think of yourself with sober judgment'. Sober judgement, as opposed to intoxicated judgement, is realistic and accurate. It is willing to praise, while it also notes areas of shortfall or challenge. It is about having your eyes wide open and being able to spot both the good and the disappointing.

While it has become unpopular to talk about sin, the Bible's most common word for sin is *hamartia*, which in the Greek essentially means to miss the target or to fall short of the mark. When sin is thought of in this way, seeing ourselves as sinners is not insulting but invitational. It is a challenging compliment, for it reminds us that we are made for more, that there are higher targets to aim at and that we shouldn't settle for second best. It invites us to step up to the mark and aim with greater focus. Those who are full of themselves assume they are on target. The modest are more willing to listen to the Bible's verdict of *hamartia* – you are not yet on target and therefore this is not the time to be complacent. The result is that the modest grow, while the overconfident underperform.

To become more modest, allow a greater number of people to speak into your life. Most of us live in echo chambers where we are surrounded by people who think and see things much the same way as we do. Be very wary if you are surrounded by people whose tastes and attitudes are inseparable from your own. They will feed your ego but will rarely contribute to your growth. The modesty of quiet leaders often sees them actively seeking feedback from people they know will see things differently. They will value their insights, knowing that better decisions are made if the alternatives are both explored and understood. Not that they will uncritically accept all feedback given. We all need to grow in self-knowledge, and while some will suggest paths we should travel, our own inner awareness will often alert us that this is not the road for us. To put it slightly differently, we should ensure we receive a wide range of feedback, but we are responsible for which recommendations we either accept or reject, for there are times when well-intentioned guidance must be ignored.

Modest leaders ask, 'What are we missing? What have we failed to see?' These reflective questions might slow the pace, but if they *are* asked, the quality of decisions made is likely to be higher.

**Restraint**

Restraint: The capacity to hold back or control an emotion or
impulse which could otherwise cause damage

While leaders should be stirrers, diving in and unsettling complacency, this needs to be tempered with restraint. Precisely because
leaders help set new paths, and the consequences of their actions can
be so far reaching, they need to engage thoughtfully and systematically. Followers deserve something more than leaders who act on
impulse, claiming their intuition is always right. Facts are friends,
and good leaders take the time to review the relevant data, and when
it does not support their proposal, they pause and investigate more
thoroughly.

Restraint also points to an ability to breathe deeply in difficult
situations and not to dump emotions on others. Leadership can be
pressured, and the stress can tip some leaders into taking their disappointment or temper out on their team. This can leave people
demotivated, depressed and angry. Sometimes a vicious spiral can
set in, and those who are unfairly blamed start to blame those below
them, who do the same to those below them. An unhealthy team
culture of 'naming, blaming and shaming' can set in.

How can we develop restraint?

Sometimes we simply need to work at it. We can make a conscious decision to delay giving the first response that comes into
our head. We can develop the art of being curious, and actively ask
why someone holds the view they do, rather than telling them why
they are wrong. We can make a decision, but then deliberately delay
acting on it until we have run it past trusted guides.

We can also develop the art of consciously delaying decisions until we have sat in a variety of seats – thinking about the implication
of a decision for the people who routinely sit there. Put differently,
we can ask: 'If I was the CFO [chief financial officer] and not the
CEO [chief executive officer], how would I feel about this?' Or: 'If I

was an elderly member of the congregation, how would I feel about this? And if I was a young person in the church?' Leaders are shepherds, and when we feel the weight of some decisions for those we shepherd, we sometimes hear God calling us back to the drawing board, gently saying to us, 'You can't just push this through. The price tag for some is too high. It's going to take more time and more careful thought.'

At another level we can learn the art of breathing deeply. Literally pause, breathe in deeply through your nose to the count of four (feel the air come in all the way to your stomach), then breathe out through your mouth – also to the count of four. This is a wonderfully calming technique. If we are in a meeting and find we are getting angry, we can intentionally call a break for a few minutes. If we are in a setting where it's appropriate, we can stop and pray.

## Tenacity

Tenacity: The ability to keep going, often in the face of difficulty and opposition

While leadership might sound glamorous, the truth is that leaders carry heavy loads. They know the buck stops with them and are conscious that people expect them to find solutions when difficult problems lie ahead. They bear the burden of the often-contradictory hopes and expectations of those who follow them. Most often they are juggling a range of issues, some of which invariably turn out to be more complex than initially thought. The temptation to give up is ever present, and most leaders I have spoken to have written their resignation letter on more than one occasion – though have then pulled back from delivering it.

Leaders succeed not because they miraculously manage to avoid problems, but because they persevere through them. How can we strengthen our tenacity?

First, expectations are important. When we know we will face difficult times, they become less difficult! While this might sound strange, if we are able to look at problems as slightly awkward but entirely expected friends, they become more manageable. A major part of any leader's job is to solve problems. When we remember this, we are a lot less thrown by difficulties that arise. They are simply part of the job. Put differently, when next you hear yourself complain that there's always a problem to solve, push back on yourself. Isn't that what leaders do? What else did you expect? If everything was simple and obvious, would your services as a leader be required?

Second, we can take ourselves a little less seriously. Leaders get criticized. It's part of the job. Better leaders listen to the criticism, run it past a few trusted friends (and not the same ones every time, for a range of views helps), adapt where necessary and discard what shouldn't be taken on board. They realize that the things people criticize them for sometimes tell them more about the person doing the criticizing than about themselves, and so they don't take it too personally. On the contrary, they are often able to listen compassionately, understanding that some people carry heavy burdens which can make them angry and unreasonable. In short, criticism might tell us something about ourselves, but it could also tell us something about the other person and make us less defensive as a result.

Third, tenacious leaders remember that tomorrow is another day. Put within a theological frame, it might be Friday, but Sunday's coming. Resurrection follows crucifixion. What matters is that we stay the course and are still around when the tide changes. We can philosophically ask: 'In a few months' time am I likely to remember this setback?' The answer is usually 'no'. While most problems seem pressing at the time, when we recognize that we are unlikely to remember them in the future, tenacity is easier and we are more likely to see things through.

An obvious question must be asked: how do we know when it is time to give up? Can tenacity sometimes lapse into a stubborn and misguided refusal to accept the inevitable, often with much greater damage resulting from the delay?

More than at other times, this current season in the church's story reminds us that leaders are not just stirrers. They also need to be saints. Spiritual leaders (with the emphasis on 'spiritual') often know deep inside their being that they must carry on. Though it sounds vague, they know because they know. Having spent years trying to be attuned to the faintest whispers of God, they hear that whisper saying, 'Don't give up. I know it's discouraging, but you are not alone and this is the right path.'

I do not want to trivialize or commodify this issue. Sometimes we are uncertain about whether to give up or not. Sometimes God gives us a clear answer, and it might be accompanied by tangible signs. But 'sometimes' is not the same as 'always'. There are occasions when we feel as though we are operating in the dark, and are not at all sure what we should be doing. At those times, I have tried to remain obedient to what I am confident I last heard God say, and I operate from the principle that if God has had a change of mind, the onus is on God to let me know. I don't say that arrogantly or impertinently, for deep in myself I know that I cannot figure out God's purposes on my own and must hold on to what I am reasonably sure I heard.

In my own experience I listen for the call of God and the release of God. When invited to a position, be it a long-term post or a role in a short-term project, I try to sense if God has written my name on it. Not too surprisingly, if the answer is 'yes', I accept, and then keep going. Tenacity is often required, but if I know that the problems I am struggling with have my name written on them, I am not overly concerned.

At times in the journey I have discerned a change, or a feeling that I have now done what I can and that the next stage in the journey has someone else's name on it. This is usually accompanied by a sense of release. It is not the time for tenacity but for handover, for it is now someone else's task to lead the group on.

This is another reminder that leaders usually shape a chapter of the overall organizational book, but they are not the whole book. To refuse to finish your chapter because you thought you were going to write the whole book is a serious and sad mistake.

In short, be tenacious, but remember there is a time to stay and there is also a time to walk away. How we walk away matters, and we should do so with dignity, trying to ensure that our successor has the best chance of success.

## Interdependence

Interdependence: The recognition of our interconnectedness, and our need for and reliance on one another

Rather than being a weakness, our need for one another is a significant strength. Some leaders are instinctively competitive. At their worst they may adopt a 'winner takes all' attitude, viewing anyone else on their patch with suspicion and resentment. While this can seem uncomplicated, with everyone working for their own interests, over time it leads to isolation, loneliness and poor overall results, for when we cut ourselves off from others we lose the benefit of their insights and friendship. Our world becomes small and lonely, a narrow compilation of those who are 'in' and those who are 'out', or a tiny world of 'them' and 'us'.

Quiet leaders are drawn towards 'win-win' thinking and are more comfortable when working cooperatively. Although they know it takes time to build relationships, they are convinced that a rich dividend will result. As trust builds between groups, they see others as collaborators, and lean towards rather than away from one another when a new proposal is made.

Naturally, some give and take is required in all relationships. While recognizing that their first responsibility is to their own group, quiet leaders know that no group is sufficient on its own and that we are dynamically interconnected to one another. In Genesis 12:3 Abram is informed that while God has chosen and blessed him, there is a wider purpose behind it. All nations of the world are to be blessed through Abram's offspring. Put differently, Abram's blessing was to overflow into a blessing for all. This is not an isolated passage, for the Bible repeats it a further six times (Gen. 18:18; 22:18; 26:4; 28:14; Acts 3:25b; Gal. 3:8). We are supposed to notice the pattern. We are blessed in order to bless. It starts when we recognize that we are interconnected. God cares about my flourishing, but then so does God care about your flourishing and the flourishing of this planet. Like it or not, we are interconnected, and will all fare better when we consciously opt for a leadership style that is inclusive, appreciative of the other, and interdependent.

How can we improve in this area? We could begin with an audit of the relationships we are in. Be honest. Are they primarily competitive or cooperative? If largely competitive, what steps can be taken to change this? You might need to be selective. Some groups are more open to cooperation than others. At times you will hear yourself say philosophically, 'I guess it's just not going to happen in this relationship.' If you hear yourself saying this all the time, you are probably rationalizing your own competitiveness, but if it is only an occasional conclusion, you are likely to be on track. Romans 12:18 is instructive: 'If it is possible, as far as it depends on you, live at peace with everyone.' It doesn't always depend on us (and some things are beyond our control), but when it does, we must live at peace with everyone. In other words, we must be happily and cooperatively interdependent.

## Other-centredness

> Other-centredness: The virtue of valuing and promoting the good of the other

Leaders who are 'other centred' go a step further than being interdependent. They take the needs of the other so seriously that they put them ahead of their own. This is servant leadership at its best. It starts with the leader realizing that it is not all about them. Sadly, many narcissists are drawn to leadership, looking to it to stroke their egos as they try to appear indispensable. They bask in the praise of their followers and quickly marginalize any who might challenge their image. Acting as a servant helps to sift out the narcissists. They quickly tire when it isn't all about their agenda.

Other-centred leaders operate differently. Their motivation is not their reputation, but the well-being of the group. They are genuinely captured by a vision that is larger than their own success, and consider leadership a privilege, not a right. They are in leadership because they have something to offer, not because of something they want to get from it.

Now life is rarely simple, and few of us operate from entirely pure motives. According to the Myers-Briggs personality inventory, I am an ENTJ – a profile which is often associated with those who lead.[6] If the profile is correct, apparently despite my quiet and relatively gentle disposition, I inevitably end up in leadership positions because I make decisions easily, am adaptable, keep the big picture in mind and am comfortable with responsibility. Put differently, I rather enjoy leading. In saying that leaders should be other-centred, I am not suggesting that they take no pleasure in leading or that they do not find it fulfilling, or that they get nothing from it. It's just that the best leaders are willing to set their own agenda aside for the good of the group. At some level, their greatest joy is when they see the group they help lead flourishing – and I say 'help lead' because we don't lead alone, even if we think we do.

When we are other centred, we remember the bigger picture of what we hope to achieve. Perhaps you are a church leader and want to see the message of Jesus spread far and wide. The truth is that you are one of many church leaders longing for a similar outcome. In the busy rush of leadership, we may forget that we are part of a larger team, a team that might benefit disproportionately from some sacrifices we could make. If we have a limited focus, we may close ourselves off to this possibility, thinking only of our patch.

Ironically, this myopic thinking backfires over time, for when you are other centred your world expands, and the gain of the other becomes your gain as well.

How might we become more other centred?

First, we need to be honest with ourselves and critically assess whether we genuinely add value to the life or work of others. We should ask who benefits the most from the leadership we exercise. Leaders often earn more than other people and have additional perks for the work they do. We need to ask ourselves whether the contribution we make to those we lead justifies the benefits given to us. If not, we should question the motivation behind our leadership.

Second, we should ask God to open our eyes to see those we should reach out to. Sometimes there are obvious ways we could help others, but we don't do so, because we neither look nor listen, and so remain oblivious to those God has put in our orbit.

## Quiet leadership: the downside

While there are many positive things that can be said about quiet leadership, it would be foolish not to address the elephant in the room. If quiet leadership has so much going for it, why do we continue to think of leaders as dynamic, charismatic figures? And why are the confident and outgoing more likely to be put into leadership roles?

If you are a quiet leader, you will have to grapple with several challenges that your louder counterparts may not struggle with – though perhaps they will, for we don't know what goes on deep inside another person and should guard against assumptions that might be false.

Here are five of the more common obstacles quiet leaders face.

1. People overlook quiet leaders and underestimate their ability. This often works the other way round as well, with quiet leaders underestimating their ability and consequently not having the confidence to step up for challenges they could easily manage.

2. The achievements of quiet leaders are sometimes attributed to their noisier colleagues. Because they do not draw attention to themselves, the contribution of quiet leaders is often glossed over or undervalued. I have seen praise given to team members who have spoken a lot but done relatively little, while the person who has quietly carried the weight of the project gets overlooked. Naturally this is unfair, but we should be realistic enough to note that it frequently happens.

3. Quiet leaders often struggle to be heard. While what they say may be valuable and insightful, sometimes no one is listening. This is why quiet leaders need to be tenacious. They need to hang in there when overlooked, and systematically work towards a different outcome next time. They might need a different strategy in order to be heard, and it is fully appropriate to think creatively about this.

4. Quiet leaders sometimes make a poor first impression. They are not into the short-term sprint and usually produce their best results over time. They look for the compounded benefits of consistency of direction and decisions. Since a lot of people are more impressed by sprinters than long-distance runners, many quiet leaders don't get as much support along the way. The cheering of the crowd is a lot softer for long-distance runners than it is for those in a 100-metre dash, so quiet leaders may need to find other sources of encouragement and affirmation.

5. Often (though certainly not always) quiet leaders are introverts, and introverts need to manage their energy thoughtfully to effectively navigate the people demands of leadership. If they don't, they will quickly feel drained and depleted. This is in no way to suggest that introverts make poor leaders. In practice, introverts are commonly better listeners than extroverts, and listening goes a very long way in effective leadership. It's not that extroverts can't listen, but their enthusiasm to take part often sees them overlook more subtle cues, which are noticed by their quieter counterparts. However, introverts need to find ways to re-energize after the high

interpersonal demands that leadership often makes, and introverted leaders often have thoughtful and strategic ways of doing this. If you are an introvert, list the ways you regain energy and enthusiasm, and ensure that they are a regular part of your timetable.

At their best, quiet leaders are convictional leaders. They see that something needs to be done, and despite the challenges they face, they rise to the task. They are in it for the long haul, knowing that the greatest leadership contributions are not made by those who burn brightly but briefly, but by those who stay the course and see their chapter through. They try to make sure that their successor faces an easier task than they did and are delighted when they hear how well they are doing. When they hear this, they are usually immersed in another leadership position, for quiet leadership is not the call of a few months but of a lifetime. Having written a helpful chapter in one position, they will go on to write a helpful chapter in another.

---

### For reflection

1. Think through the five virtues of quiet leadership and rate yourself from 1 (not at all like me) to 10 (an excellent description of me). If you rate yourself below 7 on any virtue, rather than passively accepting your ranking, devise a strategy to help you grow in this sphere.

| Virtue | Rating from 1 to 10 | How I can grow |
| --- | --- | --- |
| Modesty | | |
| Restraint | | |
| Tenacity | | |
| Interdependence | | |
| Other-centredness | | |

2. Do you see yourself as a quiet leader?
   a. If yes, how will you manage the five obstacles quiet leaders often face?
   b. If not, what can you learn from quiet leaders?

# 12

# Leading without All the Answers

We do not know what we ought to pray for, but the
Spirit himself intercedes for us . . .

Rom. 8:26

We are privileged to be invited to spiritual leadership at a time of
great change. While the past has much to teach us, it has reached its
use-by date, and we need to hear the call of the future, a call which
invites us to adopt fresh forms of thinking and to consider new options. While the future will inevitably be shaped by many aspects of
the past, wise leaders will sift through the remains of bygone eras,
carefully considering what is integral to our identity and mission,
and what is simply a reflection of a culture we have now pivoted
away from.

Phyllis Tickle has suggested that approximately every five hundred
years the church faces a 'great emergence' – a time when something
genuinely new is born which shapes the agenda for the centuries
ahead. She argues that the church is currently in such a season.[1] She
likens it to having a giant garage sale, which gives us the opportunity
to consider all the items in our house and decide which of them we
want to keep and which should be discarded. Any family that has
been through the process knows how painful it can be, and quickly
discovers who its hoarders are, and who is willing to travel light.
Sometimes tempers flare and compromises are hard to reach.

Susan Beaumont makes a similar point, albeit with a slightly different emphasis, when she suggests that the church needs leaders
who can lead in a 'liminal season', an in-between time when we

know what we are moving away from but are not yet clear about what we are moving towards.[2] While it is easy to declare that certain practices from the past will no longer work, it is far more challenging to do so when you have absolutely no idea of what *will* and have no credible suggestion of what to replace them with. It is hard to lead when you don't know where you are going and you don't have all the answers; indeed, on some days it may feel as though you don't have *any* answers.

The one great advantage of knowing your limitations is that it makes you more open to listening, and as I've noted several times, the ability to listen deeply is one of the greatest assets of a spiritual leader. Let's explore this more fully.

## Deep listening

Listening starts with a disposition of respect towards the other. It means we see the other as someone with a story worth hearing and as someone we can learn from. If we see ourselves as already having all the answers we will probably only listen partially, looking for a gap in what the other person says which will allow us to insert our pre-packaged solution. We then look on the other as a potential consumer of our services, rather than someone who has been 'fearfully and wonderfully made' by God (Ps. 139:14) and whose journey we might have the honour of participating in.

When respect is accompanied by genuine curiosity, we are well on the way to being a good listener. Rather than assuming that we know why someone has done something, or that we can guess the reason why they think as they do, we ask them, and we do so without a judgemental edge to our questioning, but rather with a desire to know and understand.

Curiosity can be cultivated, and it serves leaders well, especially in liminal seasons. It begins when we remember to look for the deeper 'why'. For example, instead of assuming that someone has told us a lie because 'That is who they are – they are fundamentally dishonest', we will be curious about the prior story, and the sense of shame that might make it difficult for our 'liar' to view the truth as a friend. Perhaps it is not a story of shame but one of fear, for some have faced terrible repercussions from little things they once got wrong. Perhaps it is not that at all, but our question has simply been misunderstood. We might not communicate as clearly as we think we do. It could also be something more troubling. They may be withholding the truth from us because they deeply distrust us and feel we have no right to know what happened. It might be easier to simply dismiss them as a 'liar', but it is unlikely to progress us far along the journey of understanding, and when we don't understand, we don't lead well – and this problem is multiplied in seasons of uncertainty.

Genuine listening often starts when we name things well. We sense that the story we have heard misses too much and that there might be a layer of meaning that needs to be unpacked by framing things differently or finding new words to describe it. Mark Strom has perceptively noted that 'new words may not change anything. But nothing changes without new words.'[3] Names open doors of possibility, which is why the first task given to Adam in Eden's garden was to name the birds and the animals (Gen. 2:19–20). In giving them a name, he was shaping the way their role in the world would be seen. No longer would he call out 'Hey animal, come here', but 'Mrs Gorilla, could you move my way?' Names and words help you to move beyond reductionistic generalizations to the features that make someone or some situation special. It is why leaders help the groups they lead to discover their voice and find fresh ways of telling their stories – ways that energize and give hope.

Our listening is often negatively impacted by the unacknowledged names we give to people and things. Though we may not say it, we often form a snap impression which sees us name them unhelpfully. To us, a person may be the 'whiner' or the 'loser' or the 'troublemaker' or the 'genius' or the 'people pleaser' or the 'timid one'. Having tidily put them in a box with our label, we are no longer open to the mystery inside them, a mystery that has been hidden by our inadequate name. When we think we have settled on someone's name, we stop helping them work towards a better one.

Though most of us would object if we were accused of being prejudiced against someone, few of us understand how bias works subtly but profoundly within us. It prevents us from listening deeply and well. Genuine openness to the other is rare, and many underperform because they have never been listened to well. We tend to rise to the level of others' expectations of us, and if that level is dismissive, we are likely to achieve little. David Augsburger has movingly written: 'Being heard is so close to being loved that for the average person, they are almost indistinguishable.'[4] One of the greatest gifts a leader can give is to see and to hear those who are following, especially if they have been given a limiting name that holds them back. Love listens carefully for what could be if things were framed differently.

Let's think a little more systematically about some common biases which prevent deep listening. While my list is far from exhaustive, here are six to mull over.[5]

1. **Confirmation bias**, where we give greater weight to ideas that sit comfortably with our own, and are dismissive of those that don't. In other words, we pay attention and listen to those views that support ideas we want to uphold, and gloss over information that challenges beliefs we have. We unconsciously listen to have our bias confirmed. I have often been intrigued by what people remember or highlight from talks I have given. Sometimes it is what in my mind has been a very minor point, but it is the one they select, often because it adds some extra weight to something they already believe. By contrast, my more provocative points are usually quietly dropped as though they were not heard, or if they were, are best forgotten. Confirmation bias means we hear what we want to hear. Naturally this works out differently if someone comes looking for a fight, in which case they hear only that which they disagree with and dispute. This is still confirmation

bias because the underlying position is a prior assumption that the other person is someone to be disagreed with, and so we listen out for our differences to confirm our hostility.

2. **Complexity bias** is present when we are more likely to be drawn towards a simple lie than a complex truth. The trouble is that life is complex, and our preference for simplicity sees us dismissing important truths. Politicians have long realized this and so instinctively steer away from genuine explanations and lean towards soundbite oversimplifications that are so generalized that they border on the meaningless. There is an old quip that a half-truth paraded as a whole truth becomes an untruth. If we are to listen deeply, we must learn the art of being comfortable with nuance and colliding truths.

3. **Confidence bias** is shown when we believe something to be true simply because someone has said it boldly and without doubt. We are more likely to believe a confident lie than a hesitant truth. This can be a challenge for leaders, for our followers often want certainty from us, but we lead in a liminal season and only the dishonest or deluded claim to know just what lies ahead. Truth comes out over time, and quiet leaders learn to be comfortable with this. Rather than posture for the short-term win, they position themselves for long-term credibility, preferring to under-promise and over-deliver than to publicly commit to deliver what people want while privately knowing that it is unlikely to happen.

4. **Complacency bias** is demonstrated when we uncritically believe something that requires no change from us and does not disturb our comfort. Listeners often long for an easy reassurance that everything is going to be fine and will approve of communicators who pamper this unrealistic desire. Better leaders know they are stirrers and should help their followers to move outside their comfort zone. They know that people tend not to see what they don't want to see, and that they must help them face inconvenient truths. There are risks in this, for we could be tempted to sensationalize the situation or elicit a response which flows from

fear. Some catastrophize situations, basically being willing to as-
sert anything to move people out of their lethargy, but credibility
is a long-term game and can be quickly lost. Wise leaders persistently point back to the facts until the need for action is seen and
owned by the group.

5.  **Cash bias** prevents most people from accepting information that
    could negatively impact their financial circumstances, especially
    if it means they would have to find a different way to earn a
    living. It is hard for us to accept uncomfortable truths, but they
    don't disappear simply because we prefer not to confront them.
    When people are likely to be financially impacted by a needed
    change, leaders can think ahead and consider viable alternatives.
    They should show that they understand the cost of change is
    real, but that endless delays often lead to a higher price tag. They
    should find a way to be with their people as they try to navigate
    these changes, and they should accept that they are unlikely to
    be exempted from the costs that others will carry and must play
    their part in shouldering the load.

6.  **Culture bias** occurs when we assume that our culture's way of
    doing things is best and poorly understand the rationale behind
    other cultural perspectives. When we overcome this bias, excit-
    ing possibilities open up. Just as our cultural bias prevents us
    from seeing some problems, it also stops us seeing opportunities
    that are more obvious when we approach things with a different
    cultural lens. The journey ahead can be rich and rewarding. It is
    sometimes said that 'we don't see what we don't see', and this is
    often a consequence of the cultural perspective we automatically
    gravitate towards. When we acknowledge our cultural myopia,
    we are in a better position to step back and ask, for example:
    'How might I approach this if I was part of an honour–shame
    culture or thought about it from a different starting point?'

Now there are many more factors that are likely to bias the way we
hear and respond to things, and they certainly don't all begin with

'c' (try gender bias), but this is a helpful start and should alert us to situations where we are likely to miss important cues or dismiss significant information because it challenges our prejudices.

The antidote to bias is deep listening, where we intentionally silence our initial responses and keep listening, remembering that it is as important to understand *why* someone says something as it is to hear *what* they say. Indeed, the 'why' often turns out to be more important, for as the French proverb says: 'To understand all is to forgive all.' No doubt there are exceptions (for leaders deal with nuance), but the overall drift is accurate. Father Gregory Boyle expressed this slightly differently when he said, 'Here is what we seek: a compassion that can stand in awe at what the poor have to carry rather than stand in judgment at how they carry it.'[6] When we make this shift, we see and hear differently, and our leadership is often radically reshaped by what we start to hear.

**Pause for a moment**

This book's focus isn't so much on leadership theory as it is on forming you for spiritual leadership. This requires some self-reflection. Think about your listening style and, in particular, the bias filters you might not have come to terms with. Rate yourself from 1 to 5, where 1 is 'I never fall into this trap' and 5 is 'I repeatedly make this mistake'.

| Bias/Rating | 1 | 2 | 3 | 4 | 5 |
|---|---|---|---|---|---|
| Confirmation | | | | | |
| Complexity | | | | | |
| Confidence | | | | | |
| Complacency | | | | | |
| Cash | | | | | |
| Culture | | | | | |

Linger over your scores of 4 and 5. Then answer these questions:

1. Why do these particular biases trip you up? Push yourself for a genuine answer (as opposed to a trite 'let's get the question over' answer).
2. Who have you hurt because you didn't listen to them properly? Is there something you need to do about this?
3. How can you avoid falling into this trap in the future?

## Generative listening[7]

Most of us prefer to be listened to than to listen. However, God made us with two ears and one mouth, and as is often noted, this is probably a clue that we should listen twice as much as we talk. Are there ways to listen that are more rewarding and might tempt us to lean in towards what others are saying, rather than impatiently waiting for our turn to dominate the conversation?

C. Otto Scharmer has suggested that there are four 'fields of listening', or places from which we listen. Let me loosely interact with his ideas, applying them to how we listen to God, to others and to ourselves, and especially focusing on his concept of generative listening, which he argues is crucial for future-focused leaders.[8]

Each of Scharmer's four fields of listening is appropriate in a particular setting. Here are the four:

1. Listening as downloading
2. Listening for the facts
3. Listening empathetically
4. Listening generatively

Roughly speaking, here is what he means by each.

## Listening as downloading

Listening as downloading, or mechanical listening, is when we listen from habit, waiting for views that reconfirm our own and filtering out those that don't. Our attention isn't really on what the other person is saying, but more on the intersection of what is said and our own agenda. Our focus is on what we will say in reply. We listen to find an entry point to introduce our own ideas, often doing so in a way that makes us sound a little cleverer than the other person. While this is the backbone of much polite conversation, downloading doesn't get us far. At best it is conventional, but it is not curious or challenging, nor is it intended to facilitate a genuine encounter with the other person. Realistically it is not about listening but about finding entry points into a conversation, and passing the time pleasantly but forgettably. Our conversation flows from opinions long formed, or we tell stories we have often told. Our lives don't really interact at any significant level, but these conversations reinforce our ideas and opinions as we hear our voice speak them out again and again.

## Listening for the facts

In factual listening, the focus or field of interest is the relevant data. We try to let the facts speak to us. It requires us to suspend judgement, to listen to the argument or the evidence, and to open our mind at least partially. This may be difficult to do at the start, because our opinion on the matter might have already been shaped (e.g. 'Anti-vaccinators are . . .'), but when we engage in factual listening, we endeavour to allow the evidence to shape our response although our prior attitudes might well determine what we allow to pass as evidence. For example, if a person expresses a view similar to ours we might allow an anecdotal recollection to pass as hard evidence, while we would require a more rigorous argument if the 'facts' were not to our liking. You've probably noticed in some conversations that select people are allowed 'get out of jail free' cards, while others are interrogated more suspiciously, and this is often about how closely their interpretation of the facts sits with our own (I don't need to grill you because I know you are right, even if you have not presented the case optimally). Factual listening is the listening of inquisitive minds. We find a topic of mutual interest and explore the data surrounding it. Through the meeting of our minds, we may become more affably disposed towards the other person (I see that we think alike). Although the meeting was factual rather than emotional, it might open doors for deeper levels of communication in the future.

## Listening empathetically

When we listen empathetically we switch from mind to heart, and hear what is said through the world of the speaker. This is the start of deeper listening, as we move out of our own world and enter the world of the other. We use our feelings, and we notice the other person more closely. We detect the emotion with which they speak. We sense what is left unsaid, what might be too difficult to say. Because words can get in the way at such times, we are careful with the words we use and will often sit in silence, simply being with the other person, rather than voiding the encounter with a deluge of unnecessary words. We hold a space for them and are respectful of how they opt to navigate it. We might prod a little in order to show we are comfortable with what is being said and are willing to go deeper, but we do so cautiously, remembering that our role is to listen well, not to set the agenda.

Empathetic listening can be a life-transforming experience – not just for the one being listened to but also for the one privileged enough to hear, and in some small way to help carry, the story of another. It is not about rushing to find solutions (for our stories are mysteries to be lived, not problems to be solved) but about ensuring that no one journeys alone. When your story is heard and held and valued by another, you are no longer isolated. For deep friendships to form, the empathy will need to go both ways. No, it won't be tidily measured out, for true care for another keeps no record of who has spoken the most, but it does mean that if you allow me into your life, I won't hold you at a distance but will be a true friend and allow you into mine as well.

## Listening generatively

Generative listening is the field of listening most often linked to Scharmer's work. It is a form of listening that allows space for something new to be born. It is, as it were, listening to the future and what we are called to become. It differentiates between our current self and our ideal self – what we would look like if we became all we have been made to be. It paints a portrait of what could be and asks what needs to be done differently to allow that self to emerge. It might be listening that I do for myself, or that someone helps me to do, or that I help someone else to do. Often it is about personal listening, though in Scharmer's work it is also about institutional listening – helping organizations to listen to the call of the future and the world they could help shape. For Christian leaders it can be eschatological listening. This is listening in the light of all that God plans for us and the universe, and asking in what way we might answer Jesus' prayer: 'Your kingdom come, your will be done, on earth as it is in heaven' (Matt. 6:9–10). It is about listening so deeply that new possibilities emerge. Put differently, we potentially generate a new future when we listen in this field.

Scharmer's work invites important questions for Christian leaders:

1. How would our church life be impacted if we moved from primarily operating in the field of 'downloading' (this is our faith;

this is what should be believed) to engaging in curious ('factual') conversations about new ways of expressing our humanity in the light of new possibilities that lie before us? How does our ancient (but ever relevant) faith speak into these new possibilities?

2. What would happen if we shifted gears from 'downloading' to 'empathy' when listening to people speaking about their struggles? Put differently, what might change if our stance shifted from 'We know what you should do. Are you going to do it?' to 'What is it like to be you? Can I walk with you for a while?'

3. What if we tapped into the empathy of God? What if we sensed what happens in the heart of God when news breaks about Afghanistan, Ukraine or Myanmar? How does God feel when another extreme weather event tells the story of our abuse of the planet that God entrusted to us?

4. What if we allowed our eschatology to be generative and we listened to the teaching of Jesus in such a way that it transformed our present practice? What would happen if, instead of our eschatology being escapist (one day we will get out of here), it shaped the way we do things now?

While you might well be reading this book alone, I would encourage you to explore these questions with others. They are critical questions for the future of the church. They are questions that spiritual leaders should be asking in this liminal season.

## Three specific challenges facing Christian leaders[9]

Those of us who are embedded in healthy church communities sometimes wonder why there are so many who are not. Put differently, at a time when it is easy to track down information about Jesus and learn about his teaching, why are so many deciding that following him has little appeal? A fair amount of the negative response can probably be put down to the negative publicity surrounding the church, with people thinking, 'Well, if that's the community Jesus founded, count me out.' But it is not just that.

If you ask me what I think the three greatest challenges facing Christians in the western world are (and I think the challenges are different in the majority world), I would say that in the western world Christianity is seen to be:

1. Intellectually vacuous
2. Morally suspect
3. Experientially empty

Let me make a brief comment on each of the above points, and on the leadership challenge they pose as we navigate an uncertain future.

## Intellectually vacuous

In many ways this is a bewildering accusation, for the intellectual heritage of the western world has been shaped by Christian thought, with theology traditionally being seen as the queen of the sciences. No book has been as widely distributed and read as the Bible, and nor has any book birthed as many publications as the Bible. Many of these are deeply reflective, intellectually rigorous – even profound. There is hardly an area of life where people have not thought through an appropriate Christian response. You name the area – be it theology, philosophy, economics, health, education, ethics or environmental care – and you will find that Christians have developed considered and thoughtful views. True, there is significant diversity in these views, but surely this is a strength, indicating that the Christian faith is no straitjacket enforcing dull and unimaginative thinking?

So why is the view that Christianity is intellectually vacuous so widespread among those who don't believe?

A large part of the answer is probably found in the highly vocal responses given to social issues by the most conservative branches of the faith. The views of fundamentalists are quickly spread, and the shallowness of some of these views is often seen to be representative of the whole. It is then only a short step to dismiss the whole Christian faith as superficial and silly. This is tragic, for the Christian faith is anything but silly.

Though Christian leaders must lead without all the answers and with only limited clarity about where they are headed, they must ensure that the voice of thoughtful Christians rises above the voice of fundamentalists in the marketplace of ideas. If they don't, Christianity will become an irritating reactionary voice stridently answering questions no one is asking.


### Morally suspect

Having shaped so much of the moral framework of the western world, it is disappointing that Christianity is viewed as morally suspect. This is a result of the many instances of sexual abuse, financial mismanagement and misuse of power in the church. The justified anger, horror and outrage that arises from these drowns out the exceptionally long list of good things that have been done in the name of Jesus.

But it is not just the abuse of privilege that is the cause. Many believe that while the ethical contribution of Christianity in the past was commendable, it has now gone beyond its use-by date. Christian ethics are portrayed as fixed and inflexible, unable to integrate or engage with new insights or a more scientifically informed view of the human condition. Many of our moral perspectives were shaped in the era of patriarchy where everything was viewed through a male lens. These assumptions are now being abandoned, and the Christian faith seems to be lacking in genuine thoughtfulness when it simply parrots back old formulas from a world long gone.

There is no inherent reason why this should be the case. Christianity has successfully adapted to many different cultures over its two-thousand-year history. Historically it has been a remarkably nimble faith, able to extract the best from each era and to incorporate evolving insights into the faith.

In the moral sphere, Christian leaders have two key challenges to rise to:

a. Our words and deeds must correspond. The chasm between what Christians proclaim and what they do must be bridged.
b. We must rediscover, reimagine and rearticulate a Christian moral vision for the twenty-first century. This will require digging deeply into the 'why' behind our Christian beliefs, which are often presented as a set of dogmatic and frozen ethical instructions. In some instances, the 'why' might work its way out in fresh and radically different directions. It will involve listening to Scripture in a new way. Indeed, it will require us to listen closely to what the Spirit is saying to the church through the Bible at this stage in the story of the church.

### Experientially empty

While deeper thinkers might voice their objections to faith in intellectual and moral terms, the majority of people have another reason. Christianity is seen to be experientially empty, or to put it more simply, those outside the church have found church services dull and do not see in what way being part of a Christian community is relevant to their life.[10]

This is incredibly sad. The psalmist instructs us to 'taste and see that the LORD is good' (Ps. 34:8). It is an invitation to experience God. We live in an age of experience, where we don't want to be observers, but participants. We are no longer content to hear how others climbed Everest. We might well plan to do it for ourselves. And why not make that trip to the South Pole . . . or at the very least, go skydiving, bungee jumping or hot-air ballooning? Calmly sitting in church pews listening to a talking head at the front doesn't hack it in an age where one adrenalin burst rapidly follows another.

Not that this should worry us unduly. While the Christian faith has never bypassed the head, it has never been intended solely for the head. Faith is meant to express itself in a life of action. For the original disciples this led to a heart-pounding adventure, one miracle after another as Christianity slowly captured the imagination of the world. But there was also one martyrdom after another. Of the original twelve disciples, only John managed to avoid death as a direct result of following Jesus (true, the death of Judas Iscariot saw other factors at play). It was for them the wildest of wild rides, and in the end, it changed the world.

There is an implicit challenge for spiritual leaders behind this third stumbling block to faith. If we want to avoid accusations of experiential obsolescence, we need to encourage a wave of genuine twenty-first-century Christ-following – taking the risk of living as if Jesus is real, still alive, and can be trusted. Whatever else this journey might be, if genuinely and seriously undertaken, it will never be dull. If it's the path we take, what better time to be a leader?

---

**For reflection**

1. Listen to the three key challenges from the position of a stirrer and a saint: intellectually vacuous, morally suspect, experientially empty.
   a. As a stirrer, what needs to change if the church is to rise above these challenges?
   b. As a saint, what are the spiritual challenges and dangers as we try to forge a new future?
2. This chapter has been rich in content. Flick back over the pages. What are the things that stood out for you? Why? Is there something you need to do? What? Ask someone to hold you accountable for your progress.

---

# 13

# Conclusion: Forming Spiritual Leaders

Ask and it will be given to you; seek and you will find;
knock and the door will be opened to you.

*Matt. 7:7*

This has been a book about forming stirrers and saints, spiritual
leaders who will guide and inspire those who follow them to dream
more boldly, live more courageously and follow Jesus more faithfully.

I wish it was possible to finish the book with an easy six-step or
seven-step plan that would guarantee successful and ethical Christian
leadership. But formation doesn't take place like that. It is an ongoing process that involves detours, discipline and heartache. It's a
slow cooker, quietly simmering away and reflecting on life's lessons,
rather than a microwave sprint to a fast but tasteless outcome. It also
involves many mistakes, for getting things wrong is often a prerequisite to getting things right, and this especially in an era when it is
not always clear what 'getting it right' looks like.

I am writing as a 66-year-old. Looking back at over half a century
of following Jesus, I ask myself if there were any shortcuts I could
have taken and what I should have done differently. Realistically you
can't put an old head on young shoulders. Often the clock needs to
have been ticking for a while before some truths sink in.

Earlier, I mentioned I was appointed principal of a Bible college
when I was 31. I quickly felt out of my depth, largely because I was.
Soon after I arrived the college hosted a supporters' evening, and as
I was circulating through the crowd I came upon an elderly woman.
After a few sentences she asked me, 'And tell me, dear, what is it that

you are studying at the college?' I tried to explain that I wasn't a student but the new principal, but she wouldn't believe me. 'Oh, you are such a joker,' she kept saying. It left me feeling rather a fraud.

Several of the students were older than I was and had a far wider life experience. Rosemary and I had two young children, and during my three years in the post we experienced a miscarriage, a serious home robbery (only some of my older clothes were left – I felt quite insulted that the burglars didn't want them!), an armed robbery of the house next to us, a car accident, the death of both our fathers, and numerous other difficult life-experiences. The college workload was enormous, partly because I was determined that we would be the best Bible college imaginable. It's hard not to be competitive when in your thirties – or at any rate it was hard for me. I got a lot of my sense of self-worth from thinking I was more successful than others, and so my drive to ensure that the Bible college achieved on all fronts was relentless. It was also exhausting. Earlier, I wrote of looking at my sleeping 3-year-old daughter one night and thinking that I risked being so busy that I would never really know her. It seemed an unreasonable price to pay. After completing two years as principal, I concluded that I needed to plan an exit strategy. It took me a year to put that insight into practice. I never regretted it.

Shortly before I left, one of the lecturers came to me and said simply: 'You didn't make a mistake in thinking that you should be a Bible college principal. It's the right post for you – but it's the wrong time in your life. Remember that when you are a little older.' I did. When I was 47, I was invited to become principal of a theological college in Western Australia. I accepted. I was there for seventeen years – seventeen excellent years. This time it was the right post at the right time. It's best not to try and fast-track some things, no matter how flattering premature invitations might seem.

Not that we should be passive about our growth as spiritual leaders. It is more that we should approach the journey with humility, allowing ourselves to be formed by the ups and downs of life.

I now head up AVENIR Leadership Institute.[1] After years of providing formal accredited training that went all the way to the PhD level, I now delight in working with emerging leaders and organizations in a more flexible way. Both accredited and flexible training have their place, and I count it a privilege to have been involved with both. What I see and hear as I meet small groups or engage in deep conversations with budding stirrers and saints is consistent.

People want to make a difference, but they don't want to burn out and are keen to find an appropriate work–life balance. They are desperate for credible role-models. They want freedom to think in new ways. They want to be allowed to make some mistakes. They want honest and authentic feedback that is both respectful and stretching. They want to be trusted. They want to be seen, and they want to see. They want to be heard, and they want to hear. They want to wake up each day with a sense of purpose, and they want to inspire others to lead purposeful lives. Money is not irrelevant, but it usually isn't the major driver.

They want to lead, and they want to lead well. They have a vision for a flourishing future, and they understand that the test of leadership is not so much what happens to the leader as what happens to those who follow their lead. They want followers to flourish and, in time, to lead as well.

Most of (though not all) the people I work with are Christians. Several are just hanging in there, deeply disappointed by some disturbing church experiences and frustrated that the church they are part of is stuck in a time bubble that isn't coming back. Others are more positive. Their local church meets their expectations. Often they are the person leading it and they are optimistic about the future.

Those who are progressing steadily have a strong sense of direction. They have a vision for their life and a clear mission that will help bring the vision to realization. They are focused, and rather than grasping after each shiny new opportunity, they know which ones have their name on them, and they steadily move forward along a consistent path. They know that the tortoise usually wins because it doesn't get distracted but keeps putting one foot in front of the other. Focus matters. And they are motivated. They have learned that there is no motivation fairy who pours out an endless supply of 'get up and go'. Rather, they know that motivation comes from doing – not any kind of doing, but doing that has a clear direction and focus. Those who sit in endless talkfests become demotivated; those in the game start getting runs, and getting runs is very motivating.

These then are the three qualities I look for in leaders: direction, focus and motivation.

But there are others, like the willingness to own their stage in the leadership journey and to learn the lessons each stage offers. Like humility and non-defensiveness. When we allow life to teach us, growth is rapid. Like being willing to have a go. Because you make a difference when you are in the game, not when you are muttering away on the sidelines.

Matthew 7:7 records Jesus as saying: 'Ask and it will be given to you; seek and you will find; knock and the door will be opened to you.' Ask, seek, knock. They are three specific actions to take.

Ask God about the direction your life should take. Anticipate a period of seeking, but be quietly confident. For those who seek will find. And don't be afraid to knock at doors. For those who do so discover how often they open – and that's when the leadership journey really begins.

So why not ask, seek and knock, and accept the invitation to be a leader who is both a stirrer and a saint? You are called to nothing less.

# Notes

## Introduction

[1] For an important exploration of this, see Scot McKnight and Laura Barringer, *A Church Called Tov: Forming a Goodness Culture That Resists Abuses of Power and Promotes Healing* (Carol Stream, IL: Tyndale Momentum, 2020).

[2] I deal with this question in far greater depth in my book *Why Christianity Is Probably True: Building the Case for a Reasoned, Moral and Relevant Faith* (Milton Keynes: Paternoster, 2020).

[3] I write in depth about quiet leadership in my book *The Tortoise Usually Wins: Biblical Reflections on Quiet Leadership for Reluctant Leaders* (Milton Keynes: Paternoster, 2013).

## 1 Formed by Life

[1] Pádraig Ó Tuama, *In the Shelter: Finding a Home in the World* (London: Hodder & Stoughton, 2015).

[2] For some helpful insights into habits and strategies for breaking them, see James Clear, *Atomic Habits: Tiny Changes, Remarkable Results* (New York, NY: Avery Penguin Random House, 2018).

## 2 Formed by Community

[1] Alan Jamieson, *A Churchless Faith: Faith Journeys beyond Evangelical, Pentecostal and Charismatic Churches* (Wellington: Philip Garside, 2000).

2 Cyprian, *On the Unity of the Church* https://earlychurchtexts.com/public/cyprian_on_the_unity_of_the_church.htm (accessed 2 Oct. 2023).

3 From an interview with Al Mohler; see Rod Dreher, 'Hauerwas: Evangelicalism Will Die from Exhaustion', *The American Conservative* (2 May 2014) http://www.theamericanconservative.com/dreher/hauerwas-evangelicalism-will-die-from-exhaustion (accessed 21 May 2018).

4 I have attempted to outline these contours in my book *The Big Picture: Building Blocks of a Christian World View* (Milton Keynes: Paternoster, 2015).

5 Scot McKnight, *A Fellowship of Differents: Showing the World God's Design for Life Together* (Grand Rapids, MI: Zondervan, 2015).

6 'Tannie' is the Afrikaans word for auntie, used in this instance as a term of endearment and respect rather than as a statement of biological relationship.

7 Donald McGavran, *The Bridges of God* (New York, NY: Friendship Press, 1955), p. 23.

8 Donald McGavran, *Understanding Church Growth* (Grand Rapids, MI: Eerdmans, rev. edn, 1970), p. 227.

## 3 Formed by Scripture and Prayer

1 Richard Foster's book *Celebration of Discipline: The Path to Spiritual Growth* (San Francisco, CA: Harper & Row, 1978) remains the classic text to study in this area.

2 N.T. Wright, *Justification: God's Plan and Paul's Vision* (Downers Grove, IL: IVP Academic, 2009), p. 37.

3 Eugene H. Peterson, *Subversive Spirituality* (Grand Rapids, MI: Eerdmans, 1994), p. 177.

4 Foster, *Celebration of Discipline*, p. 30.

5 Foster, *Celebration of Discipline*, p. 35.

6 Adele Ahlberg Calhoun, *Spiritual Disciplines Handbook: Practices That Transform Us* (Downers Grove, IL: InterVarsity Press, rev. edn, 2015), p. 72 (italics in original).

7 Foster, *Celebration of Discipline*, p. 30.

## 4 Formed by Mindfulness, Reflection and Watchfulness

1 I'm grateful to Shaun Lambert for his thoughts on attention as a muscle; see Shaun Lambert, *Putting on the Wakeful One: Attuning to the*

*Spirit of Jesus through Watchfulness* (Watford: Instant Apostle, 2016), pp. 119–21.

2  Shamash Alidina, *Mindfulness for Dummies* (Chichester: John Wiley & Sons, 2nd edn, 2015), pp. 291–9.

## 5 Formed by Conflict, Disappointment and Failure

1  Dan B. Allender, *Leading with a Limp: Turning Your Struggles into Strengths* (Colorado Springs, CO: WaterBrook, 2006).

2  For a helpful and accessible introduction to psalms of orientation, disorientation and reorientation, see Walter Brueggemann, *Spirituality of the Psalms* (Minneapolis, MN: Fortress, 2002).

3  H. Nouwen, *The Wounded Healer* (New York, NY: Doubleday, 1972).

4  Robert A. Fryling, *The Leadership Ellipse: Shaping How We Lead by Who We Are* (Downers Grove, IL: InterVarsity Press, 2010), p. 15.

5  M. Scott Peck, *The Road Less Traveled: A New Psychology of Love, Traditional Values and Spiritual Growth* (New York, NY: Simon & Schuster, 1978), p. 15.

6  Speed B. Leas, *Discover Your Conflict Management Style* (Durham: Alban Institute, rev. edn, 1997).

7  W.B. Yeats, 'Easter, 1916' https://poets.org/poem/easter-1916 (accessed 14 Feb. 2020). In public domain. First published in William Butler Yeats, *Michael Robartes and the Dancer* (Dundrum: The Cuala Press, 1920).

8  Brené Brown, 'Shame vs. Guilt', *Brené Brown* (15 Jan. 2013) https://brenebrown.com/blog/2013/01/14/shame-v-guilt (accessed 25 Feb. 2020).

9  Cited in Gil Rendle, *Quietly Courageous: Leading the Church in a Changing World* (Lanham, MD: Rowman & Littlefield, 2018), p. 11.

10  Allender, *Leading with a Limp*.

## 7 Moses: A Reluctant Leader

1  For an interesting discussion of various understandings of this event, see Avner Zarmi, 'This Week's Torah Portion: Moses Kills an Egyptian', *PJ Media* (19 Jan. 2017) https://pjmedia.com/faith/2017/01/19/this-weeks-torah-portion-moses-kills-an-egyptian (accessed 28 Feb. 2020).

2  I delivered the 2020 T.B. Maston Lecture at Carson-Newman University in Tennessee and argued that these two verses point us towards an ethic of engagement, where what we see and hear births concern, which in turn leads to situational incarnation.

## 8 Daniel: A Principled Leader

1  For my insights on how this works out in the Australasian context, see my article: 'Of Tall Poppies, Mateship and Pragmatism: Spirituality in the Australasian Context', *Stimulus* 16/3 (2008): pp. 16–20.

2  To cite the title of R.T. Kendall's book *For an Audience of One* (Lake Mary, FL: Charisma House, 2020).

## 9 Mary: A Leader from the Second Chair

1  Stephen R. Covey, *The Seven Habits of Highly Effective People: Restoring the Character Ethic* (New York, NY: Simon & Schuster, rev. edn, 2020).

## 10 What Is Leadership? A Seven 'S' Inventory

1  Kevin Kruse, 'What Is Leadership?', *Forbes* (9 Apr. 2013) https://www.forbes.com/sites/kevinkruse/2013/04/09/what-is-leadership (accessed 30 Sept. 2023).

2  C. Otto Scharmer, *The Essentials of Theory U: Core Principles and Applications* (Oakland, CA: Berrett-Koehler, 2018), p. 27.

3  Noel Tichy, *The Cycle of Leadership: How Great Leaders Teach Their Companies to Win* (New York, NY: HarperCollins ebooks, 2009), ch. 4 https://www.perlego.com/book/599133/the-cycle-of-leadership-pdf (accessed 10 Oct. 2023).

4  See for example Carol Dweck, *Mindset: Changing the Way You Think to Fulfil Your Potential* (London: Robinson, 6th edn, 2017).

5  Stephen R. Covey, *The Seven Habits of Highly Effective People: Restoring the Character Ethic* (New York, NY: Simon & Schuster, rev. edn, 2020), p. 73.

## 11 Leading Quietly

[1] Brian Harris, *The Tortoise Usually Wins: Biblical Reflections on Quiet Leadership for Reluctant Leaders* (Milton Keynes: Paternoster, 2013).

[2] See for example David Rock, *Quiet Leadership: Six Steps to Transforming Performance at Work* (New York, NY: Collins, 2006).

[3] Joseph L. Badaracco, *Leading Quietly: An Unorthodox Guide to Doing the Right Thing* (Boston, MA: Harvard Business School, 2002), p. 1.

[4] Badaracco, *Leading Quietly*, pp. 1–2 (italics in original).

[5] Badaracco, *Leading Quietly*, pp. 171–4.

[6] For a longer discussion of this, see David Keirsey, *Please Understand Me II: Temperament, Character, Intelligence* (Del Mar, CA: Prometheus Nemesis, 2006).

## 12 Leading without All the Answers

[1] Phyllis Tickle, *The Great Emergence: How Christianity Is Changing and Why* (Grand Rapids, MI: Baker, 2008).

[2] Susan Beaumont, *How to Lead When You Don't Know Where You're Going: Leading in a Liminal Season* (Lanham, MD: Rowman & Littlefield, 2019).

[3] Mark Strom, *Lead with Wisdom: How Wisdom Transforms Good Leaders into Great Leaders* (Milton, Queensland: John Wiley & Sons, 2014), p. 50.

[4] David W. Augsburger, *Caring Enough to Hear and Be Heard: How to Hear and How to Be Heard in Equal Communication* (Grand Rapids, MI: Baker, 1982).

[5] I am indebted to the work of Brian McLaren in this section, and several of the insights are his. See Brian McLaren, *Why Don't They Get It? Overcoming Bias in Others (and Yourself)* (self-published, 2019).

[6] Gregory Boyle, *Tattoos on the Heart: The Power of Boundless Compassion* (New York, NY: Free Press, 2009).

[7] Parts of this section on Scharmer's work originally appeared on my blog; see Brian Harris, '4 Fields of Listening: To God, to Others and to Self', *Brian Harris* (31 Aug. 2021) https://brianharrisauthor.com/4-fields-of-listening-to-god-to-others-and-to-self (accessed 23 Dec. 2021).

8   C. Otto Scharmer, *The Essentials of Theory U: Core Principles and Applications* (Oakland, CA: Berrett-Koehler, 2018).

9   Parts of this section on three challenges facing Christian leaders originally appeared on my blog; see Brian Harris, 'Three Challenges Facing Christians . . .', *Brian Harris* (5 Aug. 2016) https://brianharrisauthor.com/three-challenges-facing-christians (accessed 23 Dec. 2021).

10  Realistically, this is not limited to those outside the church. The phenomenon of 'churchless faith' has become common, in part because those whose faith is now churchless find church activities dull and irrelevant.

## 13 Conclusion: Forming Spiritual Leaders

1   https://avenirleadership.org.

# References

Alidina, Shamash. *Mindfulness for Dummies* (Chichester: John Wiley & Sons, 2nd edn, 2015).

Allender, Dan B. *Leading with a Limp: Turning Your Struggles into Strengths* (Colorado Springs, CO: WaterBrook, 2006).

Augsburger, David W. *Caring Enough to Hear and Be Heard: How to Hear and How to Be Heard in Equal Communication* (Grand Rapids, MI: Baker, 1982).

Badaracco, Joseph L. *Leading Quietly: An Unorthodox Guide to Doing the Right Thing* (Boston, MA: Harvard Business School, 2002).

Beaumont, Susan. *How to Lead When You Don't Know Where You're Going: Leading in a Liminal Season* (Lanham, MD: Rowman & Littlefield, 2019).

Boyle, Gregory. *Tattoos on the Heart: The Power of Boundless Compassion* (New York, NY: Free Press, 2009).

Brueggemann, Walter. *Spirituality of the Psalms* (Minneapolis, MN: Fortress, 2002).

Calhoun, Adele Ahlberg. *Spiritual Disciplines Handbook: Practices That Transform Us* (Downers Grove, IL: InterVarsity Press, rev. edn, 2015).

Clear, James. *Atomic Habits: Tiny Changes, Remarkable Results* (New York, NY: Avery Penguin Random House, 2018).

Covey, Stephen R. *The Seven Habits of Highly Effective People: Restoring the Character Ethic* (New York, NY: Simon & Schuster, rev. edn, 2020).

Dweck, Carol. *Mindset: Changing the Way You Think to Fulfil Your Potential* (London: Robinson, 6th edn, 2017).

Foster, Richard. *Celebration of Discipline: The Path to Spiritual Growth* (San Francisco, CA: Harper & Row, 1978).

Fryling, Robert A. *The Leadership Ellipse: Shaping How We Lead by Who We Are* (Downers Grove, IL: InterVarsity Press, 2010).

Harris, Brian. *The Big Picture: Building Blocks of a Christian World View* (Milton Keynes: Paternoster, 2015).

——. 'Of Tall Poppies, Mateship and Pragmatism: Spirituality in the Australasian Context'. *Stimulus* 16/3 (2008): pp. 16–20.

——. *The Tortoise Usually Wins: Biblical Reflections on Quiet Leadership for Reluctant Leaders* (Milton Keynes: Paternoster, 2013).

——. *Why Christianity Is Probably True: Building the Case for a Reasoned, Moral and Relevant Faith* (Milton Keynes: Paternoster, 2020).

Jamieson, Alan. *A Churchless Faith: Faith Journeys beyond Evangelical, Pentecostal and Charismatic Churches* (Wellington: Philip Garside, 2000).

Keirsey, David. *Please Understand Me II: Temperament, Character, Intelligence* (Del Mar, CA: Prometheus Nemesis, 2006).

Kendall, R.T. *For an Audience of One* (Lake Mary, FL: Charisma House, 2020).

Lambert, Shaun. *Putting on the Wakeful One: Attuning to the Spirit of Jesus through Watchfulness* (Watford: Instant Apostle, 2016).

Leas, Speed B. *Discover Your Conflict Management Style* (Durham: Alban Institute, rev. edn, 1997).

McGavran, Donald. *The Bridges of God* (New York, NY: Friendship Press, 1955).

——. *Understanding Church Growth* (Grand Rapids, MI: Eerdmans, rev. edn, 1970).

McKnight, Scot. *A Fellowship of Differents: Showing the World God's Design for Life Together* (Grand Rapids, MI: Zondervan, 2015).

——, and Laura Barringer. *A Church Called Tov: Forming a Goodness Culture That Resists Abuses of Power and Promotes Healing* (Carol Stream, IL: Tyndale Momentum, 2020).

McLaren, Brian. *Why Don't They Get It? Overcoming Bias in Others (and Yourself)* (self-published, 2019).

Nouwen, H. *The Wounded Healer* (New York, NY: Doubleday, 1972).

Ó Tuama, Pádraig. *In the Shelter: Finding a Home in the World* (London: Hodder & Stoughton, 2015).

Peck, M. Scott. *The Road Less Traveled: A New Psychology of Love, Traditional Values and Spiritual Growth* (New York, NY: Simon & Schuster, 1978).

Peterson, Eugene H. *Subversive Spirituality* (Grand Rapids, MI: Eerdmans, 1994).

Rendle, Gil. *Quietly Courageous: Leading the Church in a Changing World* (Lanham, MD: Rowman & Littlefield, 2018).

Rock, David. *Quiet Leadership: Six Steps to Transforming Performance at Work* (New York, NY: Collins, 2006).

Scharmer, C. Otto. *The Essentials of Theory U: Core Principles and Applications* (Oakland, CA: Berrett-Koehler, 2018).

Strom, Mark. *Lead with Wisdom: How Wisdom Transforms Good Leaders into Great Leaders* (Milton, Queensland: John Wiley & Sons, 2014).

Tichy, Noel. *The Cycle of Leadership: How Great Leaders Teach Their Companies to Win* (New York, NY: HarperCollins ebooks, 2009) https://www.perlego.com/book/599133/the-cycle-of-leadership-pdf (accessed 10 October 2023).

Tickle, Phyllis. *The Great Emergence: How Christianity Is Changing and Why* (Grand Rapids, MI: Baker, 2008).

Wright, N.T. *Justification: God's Plan and Paul's Vision* (Downers Grove, IL: IVP Academic, 2009).

## The Tortoise Usually Wins

*Biblical reflections on quiet leadership for reluctant leaders*

*Brian Harris*

*The Tortoise Usually Wins* is a delightful exploration of the theory of quiet leadership.

Written for reluctant leaders, it interacts with three key biblical images of leadership - the leader as servant, shepherd and steward - and links them with some of the key virtues of quiet leadership - modesty, restraint, tenacity, interdependence and other-centredness. The book argues that the bulk of leadership is about helping groups decide the right things to do and then getting on and doing them.

These insights are supplemented by interviews with significant quiet leaders from around the world, ensuring a rich feast for prospective and current reluctant leaders.

978-184227-787-4

## Why Christianity is Probably True

*Building the case for a reasoned, moral and relevant faith*

*Brian Harris*

Does the Christian faith lack intellectual, moral and experiential credibility?

These are the three most common accusations made against the Christian faith today. Brian Harris examines each of these arguments in turn by outlining the issue, looking at evidence against the claim before evaluating the argument as a whole.

This book explores these questions in a rigorous but accessible way. It doesn't offer easy, solve-everything answers, but it does build a cumulative case based on reason, history and experience to suggest that God probably exists, and that the Christian understanding of God could well be valid.

978-1-78893-106-9

## The Big Picture

*Building blocks of a
Christian world view*

*Brian Harris*

A firm understanding of our faith is increasingly important in a world of differing beliefs and perspectives. If we do not have the knowledge to underpin our beliefs we are in danger of appearing shallow to unimpressed onlookers. What we really need is the building blocks of faith. We need a sense of how what we believe will work out in practice.

This accessible yet thought-provoking book equips us with the key building blocks of the Christian faith. From these strong foundations, an authentic and robust Christian faith can thrive as we live and work in the secular arena.

Discover solid biblical foundations to live out a confident faith in an ever-changing context.

978-1-84227-856-7

**Overflow**

*Learning from the inspirational resource church of Antioch in the book of Acts*

*Matthew Porter*

Birthed out of The Belfrey's call in York to overflow with the presence and power of God into their locality and region with all the resources God gives, Matthew Porter shares stories of what they have been learning and how this may help the church to reach out in mission and see many come to Christ.

*Overflow* describes characteristics, structures and strategies that any community of Christ-followers desiring to reach out beyond themselves can adopt. Questions are included at the end of each chapter, with some for individual application and some to help start activating gifts in others.

Discover the God of overflow, who invites us to give away what he gives, and be encouraged to make steps to become a church of overflow, spilling out with the good news of Christ.

978-1-78893-125-0

**Mountains Move**

*Achieving social cohesion in a
multicultural society*

*Steve Bell*

Society is made up of various cultural groups trying to live together.
We aim for social cohesion, but how do we do this as society becomes
increasingly complex, aided and abetted by political correctness?

Steve Bell peels back the complex layers of our multicultural society to
reveal the inner workings of our national life. Using the metaphor of
a mountain range, he identifies the major obstacles to meaningful and
mutually respectful interaction between Christians and Muslims and
encourages intelligent Christian engagement with western culture.

It seems mountains can move, but only when grace and truth are involved in all spheres of society, as fair-minded people of all faiths and
none, learn to model the necessary attitude and actions.

978-1-78893-218-9

## The Church Who Hears God's Voice

*Equipping everyone to recognise
and respond to the Spirit*

*Revd Dr Tania Harris*

As the central feature of the Spirit's outpouring at Pentecost and the grand prize of the New Covenant, the prospect of universal access to the Spirit is a powerful but pastorally risky concept. History tells the terrible tales of abuses associated with the claim 'God told me'.

Drawing on insights from theology, history and her groundbreaking PhD research, Harris skilfully presents a comprehensive theology and pastoral strategy for how people in the church, whatever the tradition, can hear the Spirit's voice for themselves.

978-1-78893-246-2

**Authentic**

We trust you enjoyed reading this book from Authentic. If you want to be informed of any new titles from this author and other releases you can sign up to the Authentic newsletter by scanning below:

Online:
authenticmedia.co.uk

Follow us: